the new family bread book

Ursula Ferrigno

photographs by Simon Wheeler

the new family bread book

MITCHELL BEAZLEY

To Antonia, my little darling

The New Family Bread Book
Ursula Ferrigno

First published in Great Britain in 2007 by Mitchell Beazley, an imprint of
Octopus Publishing Group Limited, 2–4 Heron Quays, London E14 4JP.
An Hachette Livre UK Company.

A CIP catalogue record for this book is available from the British Library.

ISBN: 978 1 84533 238 9

Commissioning Editor Rebecca Spry
Art Director Tim Foster
Executive Art Editor Yasia Williams-Leedham
Senior Editor Suzanne Arnold
Photographer Simon Wheeler
Designer Geoff Borin
Recipe Contributor Bridget Colvin
Editor Susan Fleming
Proofreader Sands Editorial
Indexer John Noble
Production Controller Lucy Carter

Set in Trade Gothic and Bembo

Colour reproduction by Sang Choy, Singapore
Printed and bound by Toppan, China

contents

introduction

BREAD – IT'S A PLEASURE TO MAKE AND A PLEASURE TO EAT. FOR AS LONG AS I CAN REMEMBER, I HAVE FOUND MAKING AND ENJOYING BREAD ALL-ENCOMPASSING. FOR A FOOD-LOVER AND COOK, IT'S ENDLESSLY FASCINATING. THE PRIMAL INGREDIENTS CAN BE TRANSLATED INTO HUNDREDS OF DIFFERENT, DELICIOUS BREADS. SOMETHING AS SIMPLE AS MORE TIME, MORE KNEADING, OR THE ADDITION OF OTHER FLOURS CAN TRANSFORM ONE TYPE OF BREAD INTO ANOTHER.

BREAD IS WHAT ONE MIGHT CALL A BASIC FOOD, AND THE SIMPLE MIXTURE OF FLOUR, WATER, SALT, AND LEAVEN – WHICH IS ALL IT IS IN ESSENCE – IS FOUND IN EVERY SOCIETY, LARGE OR SMALL, IN THE WORLD. THOSE FEW INGREDIENTS CAN, IN COMBINATION, BE TRANSFORMED FROM VIRTUALLY NOTHING INTO SOMETHING EMINENTLY SATISFYING, WHICH SEEMS AMAZING TO ME, ALMOST LIKE MAGIC. AND WHEN BREAD-MAKING BECOMES A REGULAR ACTIVITY IN YOUR LIFE, YOU WILL PERHAPS UNDERSTAND WHY THIS FOOD IS SO INTRINSIC IN HUMAN SOCIETY: THINK OF ITS FRAGRANCE, ITS LITERAL AND METAPHORICAL WARMTH, ITS ENDLESSLY VARIED ABILITY TO PLEASE AND SUSTAIN, AND THE LOVE OF FAMILY AND FRIENDS REPRESENTED IN THE CARE AND TIME TAKEN IN ITS MAKING.

fast breads

"CARE" AND "TIME" ARE IMPORTANT WORDS IN BREAD-MAKING. MOST OF THE BREADS IN THIS BOOK ARE RELATIVELY FAST TO PREPARE AND COOK, MAKING THEM FIT EASILY INTO FAMILY LIFE. BUT BREAD-MAKING IS NEVER A TRULY FAST PROCESS; THERE ARE SIMPLY "FASTER" BREADS. IN THESE PAGES YOU'LL FIND FASTER CLASSICS FROM ITALY, FRANCE, THE UK, AND ELSEWHERE.

TYPES OF FAST BREADS

I have included lots of recipes for yeasted flatbreads and rolls, which don't take so long rising, proving, and baking as larger loaves. But there are, of course, a few classic larger loaves too. Many of the breads will benefit from being left to rise and prove for longer, and you can do that if you have time; I have given you ideas for how to make some of the breads more slowly. But most of the recipes here can be achieved – and deliciously – in less than three hours. The non-yeast breads are particularly fast.

SLOW BREADS

The best breads you can make at home are undeniably the results of a process that is anything but conventionally fast. A proper sourdough loaf could take up to four days to make – with the fermentation of the starter, the mixing, the kneading, the repeated risings, knocking backs, and proving, then baking.

Of course, an alternative to cutting down on the time spent making bread is to change your attitude to time. Bread-making may take several hours (or occasionally days), but it is not continuous time – it is little snippets of time, which anyone can fit into the busiest of days. The various manual stages of bread-making – the mixing, kneading, proving, etc – are not lengthy individually, and you can quickly learn how to make these stages fit easily into your daily life. For instance, you can mix and knead a dough last thing at night, and leave it in the fridge to rise overnight. If you knock it back before you go to work in the morning, you can leave it in the fridge throughout the day (and for up to two days), so long as you knock it back occasionally. In real time, you will have spent half an hour at first, plus a few minutes in each session of knocking back. The dough is waiting for you to bake when you need it; it will be acquiring potential flavour and texture all the time, and I think that is what I could happily call "fast" bread. Fit bread-making into your life in a sensible way, and you'll find that it doesn't take any "time" at all.

ingredients

BREAD, IN ESSENCE, IS A SIMPLE COMBINATION OF FLOUR, LIQUID, AND A RAISING AGENT SUCH AS YEAST. OTHER FLAVOURINGS CAN BE ADDED, MANY OF WHICH I EXPLORE IN THE RECIPES IN THIS BOOK – AND I HOPE THAT BY PRACTISING THE TECHNIQUES OF BREAD-MAKING AND LEARNING HOW TO INCORPORATE DIFFERENT INGREDIENTS, YOU WILL GAIN CONFIDENCE AND START TO EXPERIMENT ON YOUR OWN!

FLOUR

Flour is the main ingredient of about three-quarters of breads. The flour you choose will give the bread its character: if it's highly refined, you will have a bland loaf, but if you use organic or stone-ground, for instance, the bread you make will be much more interesting.

WHEAT FLOURS

Most common flours are made from wheat, which consists of bran, germ, and endosperm. The bran is the husk that encloses the kernel, which is the grain – the seed in a hard shell. The nutritious wheat germ is the seed of the future plant. The endosperm, the inner part of the kernel, is full of starch and protein.

There are many varieties of wheat, the most important being *Triticum aestivum* and *Triticum durum*. Types of *Triticum aestivum* are known as "hard" or "soft" wheats. "Hardness" in wheat means that the proteins in the endosperm contain a large proportion of glutenin, the main protein that forms gluten, and, as any bread-maker knows, it is gluten that gives a bread its pleasantly elastic texture. Flours made from hard types of *Triticum aestivum* are used to make bread, and soft flours are used for pastry. *Triticum durum* is literally hard, as its Latin name suggests, and is the flour most important in the making of pasta, but it is also used in bread-making and made into semolina (and thus couscous).

Plain flour (all-purpose flour in the USA) is a blend of hard and soft wheats and can be used for breads and pastries. It has less protein and gluten than the stronger flours made for bread-making.

Strong white flour, sometimes called strong bread/plain flour, is made from hard wheat, so it has much more protein and gluten than plain flour. It is very good in bread-making. Italian flours are made mostly from hard wheat and graded according to fineness: *tipo* "00" (also known as *doppio zero*) is used for fresh pasta and cakes – and occasionally breads – and *tipo* "0" is used for bread-making. In England, I use a very strong Canadian flour, made from spring wheat, which is available from good supermarkets.

Wholemeal flour is made from the complete or "whole" wheat kernel, with nothing removed. The bran and germ content makes it very nutritious but can also hinder the rising, making a much more dense bread. It can be found in a "strong" bread-making version.

Stone-ground flour is ground slowly and gently in order to produce flour that retains all the natural goodness of the whole germ. This slow-milling process only slightly warms the flour, leaving all the natural flavours and nutrients intact.

Wheatmeal or **brown flour** is made as wholemeal (*see* page 9) but with some of the bran removed. As a result, it is lighter and will produce a less dense loaf than wholemeal flour does.

Semolina, which is milled from the endosperm of durum wheat, comes in a couple of types: coarse semolina flour and fine semolina (or durum) flour. (The latter is also referred to in Italy as *semola di grano duro*.) Fine semolina flour is ground twice to achieve its fine texture. Both sorts are good for bread-making (though coarse semolina flour is usually best used in combination with strong white flour).

Granary flour (or brown malted flour) is usually a combination of wholemeal, white, and rye flours, mixed with malted grains, which give a lovely flavour, especially for bread.

Self-raising flour is plain or wholemeal flour with a chemical leaven such as baking powder added, which can be used in yeast-free breads. (You could make your own white self-raising at home simply by adding 2 level tsp baking powder to each 225g (8oz) plain flour.)

Spelt flour is ground from the grains of an ancient relative of modern wheat and it has a delicious and distinctive nutty, wheaty flavour. Spelt flour contains some gluten, which makes it ideal for bread-making; the gluten, however, is more fragile and brittle than that found in conventional wheat flour, making it easier to digest.

OTHER FLOURS

A number of other grains, pulses, and vegetables are milled to produce flour. I don't use them in this book, but flours are made from millet, rice, gram (chickpeas), quinoa, buckwheat, and potato. Most of these are low in gluten, which means they produce rather dense breads, but they are ideal for those who are intolerant of wheat or gluten. However, many of them, when used in combination with wheat flours, contribute extra flavour and nutritional value.

Rye flour, ground from the whole grains of rye, is low in gluten, so breads made from rye alone are rather dense. It can be found as dark or light flour, the dark adding much more colour and flavour to a bread. Mixtures of rye and strong wheat flours make for very tasty breads.

Corn (or, more properly, maize kernels) is ground to several textures of meal – usually coarse, medium, and fine. Cornflour, really corn "starch", is the very fine white powder used as a thickener in sauce-making (although it can be used in some cakes and biscuits). Cornmeal, which is usually yellow, can be found in a fine or coarse texture; the latter is known in Italy as polenta and is made into the Italian "porridge", also called polenta. All corn flours are gluten-free.

Oatmeal comes in various grades, distinguished by size and texture. Pinhead oatmeal is the largest. The other most common types are medium and fine and are useful in some bread – and biscuit – making. Oat does not contain gluten, but it contributes to flavour and texture when used in tandem with other bread flours.

LEAVENS

Most of the breads in this book are leavened, or raised, by yeast, but a few use chemical leavens such as baking powder (*see* pages 146–167). There are many ways of improving the texture and flavour of the finished loaf, among them using a yeast starter or *biga*. If you have time, I highly recommend you try these slower methods. You will be amazed.

YEAST

This is the most commonly used leaven in bread-making, and it comes in several forms: fresh, dried, and easy-blend. Yeast is a living ingredient, whose action in bread-making is to convert the sugars in the flours into a gas (carbon dioxide), which makes the bread rise. Because it is a living organism, yeast is sensitive to heat, and the heat of the liquid used to prepare it is crucial, as is the temperature of the place where the yeasted dough is put to rise and prove (*see* pages 21 and 25). Too much heat will kill the yeast; too little will slow down its action. Yeast will survive after activation for about 20 minutes, then it needs to be mixed with flour, which provides food for its continued existence.

Fresh yeast is best because it is easier on the digestive tract and I think it produces the best flavours. It can be bought from bakers' shops or from the bakery departments of supermarkets. It should be used up fairly quickly, although it can be stored in the fridge for a couple of days. It can also be frozen for a month.

To use fresh yeast, dissolve it in whichever body-temperature liquid is called for in the recipe you are following before adding to the flour.

Dried yeast and **easy-blend** (or instant) yeast are fresh yeasts that have been dried and are much more concentrated than fresh, with approximately twice the potency. Dried yeasts last much longer than fresh: for up to a year (preferably in the fridge). Easy-blend yeast has much smaller granules than dried yeast.

To use dried yeast, dissolve it in the body-temperature liquid called for in the recipe before adding it to the flour.

To use easy-blend yeast, mix it with the flour in the bowl. When the body-temperature liquid is added, the yeast is activated.

STARTERS

"Starters" involve an alternative way of preparing the yeast when making bread. The most effective starters are sourdough, the French *levain,* and the Italian *biga*. Sourdough is perhaps the most famous and was traditionally made by leaving a mixture of flour and water in a bowl in the kitchen or bakery for a couple of days, during which time it would ferment through the action of wild yeasts in the air. Today most sourdough breads are made with some baker's yeast involved from the start. Breads made with these starters involve quite a lot of time and planning in advance, and you may think they have no place in a book about "fast" bread. However, you could prepare your starter a day or so before making your bread and then, really and truly, you do virtually nothing until you come to mix and knead the dough. I have given a recipe for my favourite "friend in the kitchen", the Italian *biga* below.

Yeast starter or *biga* As one of my students wisely said, this starter is the "turbo" in bread, an acid base that creates a greater depth of flavour and a better crust and texture. It is incorporated at the beginning stage of any bread: add 50ml (2fl oz) of the starter to the well in the flour when you are adding the liquid and yeast.

To make a *biga* Sift 100g (3½oz) strong white flour into a large bowl and make a well in the centre. Crumble 2.5g (⅛oz) fresh yeast into 150ml (5fl oz) water at body temperature, then add it to the well in the flour and mix to form a batter like that needed for pancakes. It must be slack. Never rely on a recipe entirely: everything can vary depending on the flour used, on the humidity, and even on the altitude (*see* page 21), so use your judgment as well. Cover it with a damp cloth and leave it at room temperature. Keep dampening the cloth for 24–36 hours, but no longer. After this time, the starter will get very tangy and when you smell it, it will make your eyes water with the acidity!

A *biga* can last for at least a day in the fridge, or you can pass any leftover on to an equally enthusiastic bread-making friend. Or, as you take some *biga* out to use in a recipe, you can feed the *biga* with more flour and a small quantity of yeast. This will feed the yeast so that it is always ready for use.

Please note that you will still have to add yeast to your recipe, even if you are using a starter. And if you find there is slight separation in the starter after a day or so, don't be alarmed: simply stir it back together.

Sponge This isn't strictly speaking a starter, but it is a technique involving fresh or dried (but not easy-blend) yeast, which helps the bread along much as does a more conventional starter. Follow the initial steps of whichever dough recipe you are using – mixing the flour and salt, then adding the yeasted water. Draw just enough of the flour into the liquid in the well to form a soft paste, then cover it with a clean tea towel and leave it for 20–60 minutes, until the paste is frothy. Even as short a time as 20 minutes allows the yeast to ferment a little, which will improve the texture and flavour of the bread. A "fast" starter! Then incorporate the rest of the flour and continue with the recipe.

CHEMICAL LEAVENS

Chemical leavens were not properly discovered and perfected until the middle of the 19th century, but they are the primary ingredient in fast breads. The combination of chemicals, when wetted, creates

carbon dioxide (as does yeast), but it does it instantly, rather than needing rising and proving time. However, as soon as the bubbles form in the dough, the bread must be baked.

Chemical leavens lose their power in storage, so they must be used fairly soon after you buy them.

Baking powder or baking soda is a ready-prepared combination of alkali and acid. Bicarbonate of soda is the alkali, which, when mixed with an acid substance, effervesces, producing carbon dioxide. This acid is usually tartaric acid or cream of tartar, an acid salt, but it can also be something such as lemon juice.

LIQUIDS

Liquid is vital in bread-making. If it is at the right temperature, it activates the yeast and starts the whole process of leavening. Without liquid, the flour could not be made into a dough. Water is the most common liquid and I prefer to use spring or bottled still waters; these contain fewer additives and are generally lighter and more pure than tap water (London water may be fine to drink, for instance, but it has a flavour and this will affect bread). Other bread-making liquids include milk, buttermilk, yogurt, and even beer and wine occasionally and all give a dough its unique consistency, texture, and flavour.

Water should be added to yeast at around body temperature: 37°C/98.6°F. You can use a thermometer for this, but an easier way is to mix two-thirds cold water with one-third boiling water.

SALT

Salt is primarily used in breads to give flavour but it also has another important role to play. It inhibits yeast fermentation, which strengthens the developing gluten, making for a better bread that lasts longer. Use natural sea salt for the best flavour (which won't complicate the bread with the extra additives a free-running salt would have). I use a fine sea salt, but if you can find only coarse (which is useful for a bread topping occasionally), crush it with a mortar and pestle.

SUGAR

Sugar used to be important in bread-making because it was used as a "food" for the yeast, but modern yeasts do not require sugar to become active. Sugar – usually granulated – is still used, though, even in savoury breads, because it enhances flavour, texture, and the colour of the crust. Honey, maple syrup, treacle, and molasses can substitute for sugar in some breads.

ENRICHING INGREDIENTS

Fats such as butter, oils, milk, and eggs are the primary bread-enriching ingredients. Fat coats the gluten strands in the dough, which slows down yeast fermentation, making for a better bread with a better flavour that lasts longer. Enriched breads are usually softer in crumb and can even be quite cake-like, depending on the amount of butter and eggs used.

Use the best possible enriching ingredients: good olive oil, preferably extra virgin; a single vegetable oil such as sunflower or safflower; unsalted butter; and fresh, large, preferably organic eggs.

bread-making techniques

MIXING AND KNEADING ARE QUITE DIFFERENT TECHNIQUES. MIXING IS THE FIRST STAGE, WHEN YOU ARE BLENDING THE BASIC INGREDIENTS TOGETHER TO A DOUGH, WHICH YOU ONLY THEN KNEAD. KNEADING IS REALLY GOOD, BLOOD-PUMPING, CARDIOVASCULAR EXERCISE THAT DISTRIBUTES THE YEAST AND DEVELOPS THE GLUTEN. IT HELPS GET RID OF THOSE "CHICKEN WINGS" UNDER YOUR ARMS, TOO, SO IT IS GOOD FOR YOU AS WELL AS YOUR BREAD.

MIXING

Measure the ingredients carefully, because the correct proportions are crucial. A good set of scales is essential. You also need a large bowl (preferably glass, so that you can see what is happening more easily) and a good wooden spoon.

Combine the flour and salt in the bowl and make a well in the centre with the wooden spoon. Pour the yeasted water (usually only a proportion of the water specified) and any starter into the well. Start to draw the flour in from the sides of the bowl, mixing with the liquid, until you have a stiff paste. Before mixing in all the flour, you can leave a paste in the well to "sponge" (*see* page 13).

Gradually pour in, bit by bit, a proportion of the remaining water, still mixing in the remaining flour from around the well. The texture of the paste will loosen, but be careful with the water additions. You don't want the dough to be too wet, and so much can affect the ability of the flour to absorb liquid. Some flours will absorb liquid more readily than others and on a humid day a flour will absorb less liquid than it will on a dry day. Never add all the liquid at once.

Mix, adding water only until the consistency of the dough is as specified in the recipe – usually firm, soft, or "raggy" (rough-textured), not sticky, but not too dry; damp is probably best.

KNEADING

Kneading enables the yeast to be distributed evenly throughout the dough and also helps the proteins in the flour to develop into gluten. The starches in the flour are broken down, these feed the yeast, and then the bubbles of carbon dioxide created by the yeast help the dough to rise. As a general rule of thumb, the more you knead, the less flavour a bread will have, but, ironically, every bread needs to be kneaded.

Bought bread (or bread made in an electric machine) is never kneaded; it's just mixed. That is why it is less digestible: because the proteins are not distributed well enough in the dough. There will be none of that familiar "bloating" if you eat home-made bread that has been kneaded well before baking.

Your work surface needs to be lightly floured – what the industry calls "bench flour". You could keep a little pile of flour to the side, just in case you need more.

FIRM DOUGHS

Put a firm dough on the surface and fold it in half toward you. Using the heel of your hand, push the dough away from you, at the same time using your other hand to rotate it slightly toward you. Continue this folding, pushing, and rotating – and adding a little more flour if the dough is sticky – for the kneading time specified in the recipe, usually about 10 minutes. The dough will change texture, becoming firm, smooth, silky to the touch, and elastic. You could try the stretch test to see if the dough is ready (*see* right). Then shape it into a ball for rising (*see* page 21).

SOFT, RAGGY DOUGHS

Doughs that are softer and damper need a slightly different treatment. Flour the board as above, perhaps a little more generously, and use a plastic dough scraper to turn the dough (your hands would get impossibly sticky). The dough will remain soft and pliable after kneading but will have lost its stickiness. This "kneading" allows the bread to be lighter when it is baked, which means it is lighter on the digestion.

KNEADING IN OTHER INGREDIENTS

Many of the breads in this book contain coarser ingredients that need to be added later than the mixing stage. These include chopped nuts, vegetable purées, spice seeds, and dried fruit. Knead the bread for a few minutes, then leave it to rest for another few minutes. Press the dough into a round and top it with the ingredient(s) to be included. Fold the dough in half, then gently knead it until the added ingredient is evenly distributed. The dough will look a bit crumbly at one point but it will come together smoothly after about 3 minutes' kneading. Or you could "chafe" the ingredients in (*see* page 22) just before proving, which I think gives a lighter texture than kneading.

STRETCH TEST

To check whether a dough has been kneaded enough for the gluten to develop elasticity, stretch a largeish piece of it between your fingers. It should behave like a piece of blown bubblegum and be thin, even, translucent, and not ripping or breaking. This is what I call the stretch test and is vital when making breads. Some people call it the windowpane test, meaning that you can stretch the dough enough, without it breaking, to enable you to see through it.

RISING

The speed of rising will depend on temperature and humidity as well as on factors such as type of flour and starter (if any). Dough will rise faster on a warm, humid day than on a cool, dry one, for instance. A warm to cool kitchen, away from draughts, is the best. But on a very hot day, you might need to put a rising dough in a cooler environment – a cold larder or the bathroom, for instance, or even the garage! On a very cold day, you could put the bowl of dough near a central-heating radiator, near the boiler, or in the linen cupboard. Mary Berry sometimes puts her bread doughs to rise on the back of her Aga (near the simmering plate rather than the boiling plate).

Altitude can make a difference, too. Really fast bread could be made at high altitudes: above 1,000m (3,500ft), a low atmospheric pressure causes bread dough to rise and prove more quickly than is indicated in many conventional recipes. Even if you live in a fourth-floor flat, you might have to revise the timings of a recipe for much the same reason.

Put the dough in a glass bowl that is large enough to allow the dough to double in size (metal is not suitable because it might conduct too much heat). Cover the dough and leave it to rise for the time recommended in the recipe you are following. A damp tea towel is usually ideal, but now and again you might need something warmer, such as clingfilm. Because clingfilm is so impermeable, if you stretch it across the top of the bowl it will speed things up, encouraging the yeast to reproduce more speedily. But be careful: clingfilm creates such a warm environment, trapping everything inside, that dough can overdevelop.

When the dough is ready, it will have visibly doubled in size and there will be air bubbles on its surface. To check that rising is complete, press a finger into the middle of the dough: the indentation will spring back slowly if the dough is ready; immediately if the dough is under-risen; and it won't spring back at all if it is over-risen.

You can put a dough to rise in the fridge, where it will adapt to the cooler temperature, giving a very slow but very even rise and encouraging flavour. This is a prime example of how you can make bread-making fit into your own life, saving precious time. But you must bring the dough back to room temperature before baking it, during which time it will puff up even more. A cold dough put straight into the oven would produce a heavy and dense bread.

KNOCKING BACK

"Knocking back" means deflating the dough to get rid of trapped gas. If this gas produced by the yeast were to carry on growing, the dough would eventually collapse. Knocking back enables the process to begin again, all the time improving flavour and strengthening crust and crumb.

Press down into the dough with your knuckles and it will visibly diminish in size. Turn it out onto a lightly floured work surface and knead it as recommended in the recipe you are following, then leave the dough to rest and relax for a few minutes before shaping and/or proving it.

One of my best-ever focaccias came about when I had no time at all. I had made the dough, but just couldn't find a minute to bake it, so I kept on knocking it back, letting it rise, then knocking it back again. I think I went on like this for a couple of days and the flavour and texture, once the dough was baked, were incredible. If you are not ready to bake, the dough will wait, so long as you keep knocking it back. Let it fit into your life, not the other way around.

CHAFING

To chafe, apply a light, downward pressure to the sides of the round ball of dough while simultaneously rotating the dough continuously in a steady, clockwise motion. This lightens the bread, expanding and lengthening the bubbles of air in it – it's particularly effective with focaccia. After a good chafe, a cross-section of baked bread will have a honeycomb-like texture. Chafing should also be used when you need to incorporate added ingredients into a dough (walnuts, for instance; *see* page 18). It will encourage your bread to be lighter and will also help distribute the ingredients more evenly. Put the ingredients on top of your ball of dough, press them in slightly, then chafe them in.

SHAPING AND PROVING

When the dough has been knocked back and rested, it is ready to be shaped and proved.

SHAPING LOAVES

Round loaf Cup your hands around the risen and knocked-back ball of dough and press your fingers into its base. Rotate the dough, applying pressure with your cupped hands to shape it into a round. Continue until you have a smooth, round shape. If you turn the dough over, there should be an indentation in the centre when it is ready. Place it on the baking tray.

Oval loaf First, create a round as above, then cup your hands around the loaf and apply pressure until you have a torpedo shape.

Long loaf Press the risen and knocked-back ball of dough into a flat round. Fold one edge of the dough into the centre. Fold the other half on top. Seal the folds on the three edges of the loaf. In the centre of the long side of the dough, press to make an indentation all the way along. Roll it under your palms until you have the desired length.

Couronne (crown loaf) Shape the risen and knocked-back dough into a round, then flatten it. Use the heel of your hand to press an indentation into the centre of the dough, right down to the work surface. Push your hands into the indentation and through to the work surface, and slowly push the dough out, using the backs of your hands to create a ring shape about 20cm (8 inches) across.

SHAPING ROLLS

Round rolls Divide the risen dough into small pieces, just large enough to fit in the palm of your hand. Roll each piece of dough on a floured surface, pressing out the air, until you have a round.

PROVING

This is the final rise, in a prepared tin or on a prepared baking sheet, which is done after the dough has been shaped (and during which time you can preheat the oven). The temperature should be similar to that of the first rising: warm to cool and draught-free. Leave the dough for the recommended time but no longer, because you do not want it to over-prove, which can be disastrous. When the dough is ready, it will have visibly increased in size and will feel spongy rather than firm. A finger indentation will spring back slowly. The dough is now ready to be glazed or topped (if not already done) and then baked.

GLAZING AND TOPPING

Bread and rolls are usually glazed after proving, but sometimes it is done before; follow the instructions in the recipe you are using. Occasionally glazes are applied before and after baking, and some toppings are added halfway through baking. The glaze is often needed as a glue for the topping. It all depends on the effect desired.

GLAZES

Glazing before baking adds colour, flavour, and potential texture to the crust; glazing after baking adds colour and flavour and usually softens the texture of the crust.

If you are glazing the loaf before baking it, put your chosen glaze in a small bowl and paint it onto the top surfaces of the unbaked, proved bread or rolls using a soft pastry brush. If you are glazing after baking, apply the glaze in the same way, while the bread is still warm.

Possible glazes include: water, milk, egg, milk and egg, egg yolk and salt, milk and sugar, honey, golden syrup, maple syrup, salted water, and olive oil.

TOPPINGS

Toppings are a delicious extra for breads and rolls, sometimes echoing the ingredient that has been kneaded in and sometimes introducing a new texture and flavour. Toppings can also make bread and rolls look more interesting. Remember that, to adhere, most toppings should be put onto a glaze.

Possible toppings include: extra flour, coarse sea salt, whole or ground spices (paprika, cumin, poppy, and sunflower), fresh herbs, grains (cracked wheat, bran flakes, rolled oats, and cornmeal), grated cheese, chopped nuts, sugars, and chopped dried fruit for sweet breads.

BAKING

You should "know" your oven – where it is hottest and where it is coolest. This will help you work out whether the shelf should be higher or lower, or whether the bread needs to be turned around halfway through cooking

PREPARING THE OVEN

First, preheat the oven to the right temperature. This probably needs 20 minutes or so and can be done while the bread is proving.

Steam There are some techniques that can help particular breads. Steam plays an important role in baking many breads: it helps soften the crust initially, helping it to rise more, and also helps it to become golden brown. There are a couple of ways in which steam can be created. You could spray the sides of the preheated oven with a water sprayer as you put the bread into it (and do so a couple of times during the baking). Or you could put a roasting tin with a film of water or a couple of ice cubes in it on the base

of the oven. Don't add any more water – this will steam the bread too much and make the crust far too soft (sometimes virtually no crust). Put the roasting tin into the oven a few minutes before you add the bread.

Preheating trays/tiles/pizza stones Many breads respond best when baked directly on a heat source, such as a preheated baking tray or sheet or a preheated ceramic tile. The pizza is a case in point: the base becomes very much more crisp when it is cooked on a preheated pizza stone.

PREPARING THE PROVED DOUGH

Slashing, cutting, or prodding a dough is done for decorative and functional reasons. If you cut or slash, you allow the bread to rise and expand without tearing elsewhere – and you also get more crust, which I think is always to be desired!

A scalpel (you can get them from kitchen or art suppliers) is a good, clean blade to use. Otherwise, use a pair of sharp scissors.

PUTTING DOUGH INTO THE OVEN

Put your baking tin or sheet into the preheated oven and close the door quickly. In the first few minutes of baking, the oven's heat turns the moisture in the dough into steam, causing the loaf to rise rapidly. The heat then deactivates the yeast, which allows the crust to solidify and become golden.

Follow the recommended baking times carefully (depending on your oven, of course) and keep an eye on the bread: if it is browning too much on one side, turn it around. Try not to open the door too much, though. That said, when you are baking rolls, opening the oven door slightly for the last 5 minutes sometimes makes the rolls crisper.

TAKING BREAD OUT OF THE OVEN

The first thing to do is test that the bread is done –
if, of course, it is not in a tin. Tap the base with your
fingertips. It should make a hollow sound.

Place the bread or rolls on a wire rack. If the
loaf is in a tin, turn it out onto the rack to cool –
the crumb will collapse if it's left inside the tin with
steam and become gooey, almost like raw dough.

And do try to leave the bread to cool. I know
it's tempting, but I don't think it's very good for
us to eat bread that is too warm. Bread is also easier
to cut when it is cooler.

STORING AND FREEZING

Make double quantities of any dough and freeze
half of it for up to six months. Most breads are eaten
straight away, but you can freeze them (whole or in
portions): wrap them in foil or special freezer bags
(get rid of air first) and seal them well. You can then
defrost the bread naturally or in the microwave – and
there you have "fast" bread.

To keep bread at home, wrap it in brown paper
and store it in a bread bin or crock. You can also keep
it in the fridge, but I don't particularly like cold bread.

You can also freeze fresh yeast, but make sure you
defrost it throughly before use (it will become liquid).
Use double quantities in exactly the same way as you
would with unfrozen fresh yeast.

BREAD-MAKING MACHINES

A bread machine can mix, rise, and bake a loaf. Many
manufacturers will tell you that it kneads the bread,
too, but no machine can stretch the dough as the
human hand can. However good the paddles of a
mixer, all they do to a dough is mix it rather than
knead it, and kneading is vitally important – as you
will find out. Consequently, machine-made bread
tends to be more dense because the gluten hasn't
been fully stretched. If your hands are in good repair,
you don't need to use a machine – and think what a
good workout you will have from all that kneading!
A second problem is that an electric bread-maker
steams a bread rather than baking it.

Most of the recipes in this book can be made
using a bread machine, but you need to use either
a yeast made especially for bread machines or an
easy-blend yeast. There are many types of bread
machines, and the order in which you add the
ingredients to the machine depends on the type
you have. Add the ingredients to the baking
cylinder and then put it inside the machine,
choose a setting, and flick the start switch.

After the machine has been kneading for
10 minutes, check the dough. Add a little water if it
is too soft; add a little flour if it is too stiff. Add any
extra ingredients, such as peel or nuts, shortly before
the end of the kneading stage.

Close the lid when the rising begins and leave
it closed until the loaf is baked. Then turn the loaf
out of the tin and leave it to cool on a wire rack.

classic breads

THE BREADS IN THIS CHAPTER ARE THOSE THAT ARE MOST EASILY RECOGNIZED AND, ON THE WHOLE, THEY ARE SIMPLE, STRAIGHTFORWARD RECIPES. THESE BREADS CAN ACCOMPANY AN ARRAY OF DAILY DISHES AND SERVE A MULTITUDE OF PURPOSES. SOME OF THEM MAY TAKE TIME TO MAKE, BUT (AND THIS IS A RECURRING THEME OF THIS BOOK) THE INDIVIDUAL STAGES OF BREAD-MAKING — THE MIXING, KNEADING, PROVING, AND SO ON — ARE NOT LENGTHY AND YOU WILL QUICKLY LEARN HOW TO MAKE THESE STAGES FIT EASILY INTO YOUR DAILY LIFE.

THESE ARE THE BREADS THAT I THINK YOU WILL RETURN TO MOST OFTEN AND, ONCE YOU HAVE MASTERED THEM AND GAINED CONFIDENCE (A VITAL ELEMENT OF BREAD-MAKING), YOU MAY BECOME INCLINED TO EXPERIMENT AND TRY ADAPTING THE RECIPES WITH YOUR OWN IDEAS — ANOTHER HUGELY IMPORTANT FACTOR IN BREAD-MAKING.

THERE ARE MANY DIFFERENT TYPES OF BREAD HERE, FROM BRITAIN, FRANCE, AND, OF COURSE, ITALY, WITH SOME "INTERLOPERS" FROM THE USA AND THE MIDDLE EAST. I HOPE YOU ENJOY THEM ALL.

pain de campagne

BLENDING DIFFERENT FLOURS CAN CREATE GREAT TEXTURES AND FLAVOURS, AND THIS BREAD IS A CLASSIC EXAMPLE. THE RYE FLOUR, FOR INSTANCE, STARTS TO FERMENT SLIGHTLY AS IT RISES, GIVING FLAVOUR AND A GOOD CRUST. MOST FRENCH COUNTRY LOAVES ARE MADE WITH A STARTER (*SEE* VARIATION BELOW), BUT THIS WORKS WELL WITHOUT.

400G (14OZ) STRONG WHITE FLOUR

115G (4OZ) RYE FLOUR

1 TBSP FINE SEA SALT

55G (2OZ) UNSALTED BUTTER, SOFTENED
    AND DICED

25G (1OZ) FRESH YEAST, CRUMBLED

300ML (10FL OZ) WATER AT BODY TEMPERATURE

1 Put the flours and salt into a large bowl and rub in the butter until the mixture resembles fine bread crumbs. Cream the yeast with 2 tbsp of the water in a small bowl. Make a well in the centre of the flour and add the yeast and enough of the remaining water to make a soft dough.

2 Tip the dough out onto a lightly floured surface and knead for 5 minutes, until it is smooth and elastic. Place it in a lightly oiled bowl, cover with a damp tea towel, and leave to rise for 1 hour, until doubled in size.

3 Knock the dough back, tip it out onto a lightly floured surface, and knead for 2–3 minutes. Shape it into a ball, then slightly flatten the top and dust with flour. Using a sharp knife, mark out a square on top of the dough. Place it on a greased baking sheet, cover it with a damp tea towel, and leave to prove for 1 hour until it has doubled in size. Preheat the oven to 220°C/425°F/gas mark 7.

4 Bake the loaf for 25–30 minutes until it is golden brown and the base of the loaf sounds hollow when tapped with the fingertips. Cool on a wire rack.

slow variation

You could make this loaf with a starter for enhanced flavour. Add a ½ recipe *biga* (*see* page 12) to the well in the flour with the recipe yeast and water, then continue as described above.

classic white loaf

THIS IS A CLASSIC BRITISH WHITE LOAF, MADE WITH MILK FOR A SOFTER CRUMB. IF YOU LIKE, YOU CAN MAKE ABOUT SEVEN CUTS IN THE TOP AND BRUSH IT ALL OVER WITH AN EGG-AND-WATER GLAZE. THEN YOU CAN SCATTER OVER A COMBINATION OF SESAME, PUMPKIN, AND SUNFLOWER SEEDS.

450G (1LB) STRONG WHITE FLOUR

2 TSP FINE SEA SALT

1 TBSP CASTER SUGAR

55G (2OZ) UNSALTED BUTTER, SOFTENED
    AND DICED

15G (½OZ) FRESH YEAST, CRUMBLED

300ML (10FL OZ) FULL-FAT MILK
    AT BODY TEMPERATURE

1 Lift the flour and salt into a large bowl and stir in the sugar. Rub in the butter until the texture is like bread crumbs, then make a well in the centre. Cream the yeast with 2 tbsp of the milk, then pour it into the well in the flour, along with enough of the remaining milk to mix to a smooth and elastic dough.

2 Knead the dough on a lightly floured surface for 5 minutes, until it is smooth. Leave it to rise in a lightly oiled bowl, covered with a damp tea towel, for 1 hour or until it has doubled in size.

3 Preheat the oven to 200°C/ 400°F/gas mark 6, and lightly oil a 900g (2lb) loaf tin.

4 Knock the dough back, then turn it onto a lightly floured surface and knead it for 5 more minutes. Roll the dough into a round, cupping your hands around the sides, and ease it into the prepared tin. Cover with the tea towel and leave to prove for 10 minutes.

5 Dust with extra flour and bake for 30–35 minutes, until the loaf is golden. Turn it out of the tin and cool it on a wire rack.

variation

You can make the dough into rolls, which are traditional and great served at teatime. After knocking back, divide the dough into 12 equal pieces and shape it into balls. Space them well apart on an oiled baking sheet, and bake for 20–25 minutes.

classic granary loaf

THIS IS CLASSIC, EASY, QUICK, AND DELICIOUS. EAT IT WITH SOUP OR TOASTED FOR BREAKFAST, OR USE IT TO MAKE SANDWICHES. YOU CAN ALSO USE IT TO SUPPLY CRUMBS FOR USE IN THE BROWN-BREAD ICE CREAM ON PAGE 187.

1 Put the flour and salt into a large bowl and make a well in the centre. Cream the yeast with 1 tbsp of the milk and water. Pour into the well in the flour and mix until the dough comes away from the sides of the bowl.

2 Tip the dough out onto a lightly floured surface and knead for 5 minutes, until it is smooth and elastic. Place the dough in a lightly oiled bowl, cover with a damp tea towel, and leave to rise for 45 minutes in a warm place, until it is doubled in size.

3 Preheat the oven to 220°C/ 425°F/gas mark 7.

4 Knock down, then turn the dough out onto a floured surface and knead once more for 5 minutes. Shape the dough into a round and place on a greased baking sheet. Brush the surface of the loaf with water and sprinkle over the porridge oats. Cover with a tea towel, and leave to prove for 15–20 minutes.

5 Bake the bread for 15–20 minutes, until it is golden and the base of the bread sounds hollow when tapped with the fingertips. Cool on a wire rack.

variation
You can make granary rolls from this dough. Divide the dough into 12 pieces and form into rounds (or whatever shape you like). Bake for 10–12 minutes.

DOUGH

450G (1LB) GRANARY FLOUR

2 TSP FINE SEA SALT

15G (½OZ) FRESH YEAST, CRUMBLED

300ML (10FL OZ) MILK AND WATER,
    AT BODY TEMPERATURE, MIXED

TOPPING

1 TBSP WATER

1 TBSP WHOLE ROLLED PORRIDGE OATS

classical focaccia

FOCACCIA GETS ITS NAME FROM THE LATIN WORD FOR "HEARTH", *FOCUS*. THIS RECIPE TOOK THE LONGEST TO RESEARCH. THE FOCACCIA I MADE AS A TEENAGER WAS MUCH SIMPLER BUT THIS ONE HAS IMPROVED ENORMOUSLY. THIS IS DUE PARTLY TO EXPERIENCE AND PRACTICE, AND PARTLY TO UNDERSTANDING THE CHEMICAL PROCESSES INVOLVED. ALTHOUGH IT'S SLIGHTLY MORE COMPLICATED AND LENGTHY THAN THE FOCACCIA ON PAGE 36, I HOPE YOU LIKE IT.

1 Mix the flour and salt in a large bowl and run your hands through the flour to warm it a little. Make a well in the centre. Dissolve the yeast in 2 tbsp of the water and add this to the well, along with 1 tbsp of the oil and the *biga*. With a wooden spoon, add the remaining water little by little, until you get a raggy dough that is not too wet and not too dry.

2 Turn the dough out onto a lightly floured work surface and knead well for 10 minutes. Use the stretch test (*see* page 18) to check that it is ready. Return the kneaded dough to a clean, oiled bowl and rub a little oil on top of it. Cover with a damp tea towel, and leave to rise for 1¼ hours.

3 Uncover the dough, knock back, and knead for 5 minutes. Cover again with the damp cloth and leave to rest for 10 minutes.

4 Roll the dough out into a round or square at least 1cm (½in) thick. Place it on an oiled baking sheet, cover with the damp tea towel, and leave to prove for 30 minutes.

5 Preheat the oven to 200°C/400°F/gas mark 6.

6 Using your fingertips, dimple the dough, then sprinkle it with coarse salt and pepper and the rosemary. Leave to rest for 10 minutes.

7 Bake the dough in the middle of the oven for 30 minutes, until golden brown. Remove from the oven and place on a wire rack to cool. When it is cool, anoint it with the finest extra virgin olive oil, cut into wedges, and enjoy.

DOUGH

250G (9OZ) STRONG WHITE BREAD FLOUR

2 TSP FINE SEA SALT

10G (¼OZ) FRESH YEAST, CRUMBLED

APPROX. 200ML (7FL OZ) WATER AT
    BODY TEMPERATURE

OLIVE OIL

3 TBSP *BIGA* (*SEE* PAGE 12)

FINISH

COARSE SEA SALT

COARSELY GROUND BLACK PEPPER

LEAVES FROM 2–3 SPRIGS FRESH ROSEMARY

EXTRA VIRGIN OLIVE OIL

simple focaccia

THIS SIMPLER VERSION OF THE CLASSIC BREAD ON PAGE 35 IS FOUND THROUGHOUT ITALY AND VARIES FROM REGION TO REGION BY THE ADDITION OF A SIMPLE SEASONED TOPPING OR A FILLING. THIS ONE IS TOPPED SIMPLY WITH CRUSHED GARLIC AND ROSEMARY AND IS MY FAVOURITE. IT IS TRADITIONALLY EATEN AS A SNACK.

DOUGH

225G (8OZ) STRONG WHITE FLOUR

1 TSP FINE SEA SALT

15G (½OZ) FRESH YEAST, CRUMBLED

185ML (6½FL OZ) WATER AT BODY TEMPERATURE

OLIVE OIL

FINISH

1 GARLIC CLOVE

COARSE SEA SALT

2 TSP DRIED ROSEMARY

1 Put the flour on a clean working surface. Gently mix in the salt, then form into a mound with a well in the centre. Cream the yeast with 3 tbsp of the water. Pour the yeast liquid into the hollow in the flour and carefully fold the flour over it, then add 3 tbsp of the olive oil. Add enough of the remaining water to make a stiff but pliable dough.

2 Knead the dough on a lightly floured surface for 10–15 minutes. Put it in a lightly oiled bowl and cover with a damp tea towel. Leave it in a warm place for about 30 minutes, until it has doubled in size.

3 Preheat the oven to 220ºC/ 425ºF/gas mark 7. Brush a baking sheet with some of the olive oil. Peel and crush the garlic and steep it in about 1 tbsp of olive oil.

4 Knock the dough back, then knead it for 2–3 minutes on a lightly floured surface. Roll out to a round about 5mm (¼in) thick. Place the dough on the oiled baking sheet. Brush the garlic and oil onto the dough and sprinkle with coarse sea salt and dried rosemary. Cover and leave to prove for 10 minutes.

5 Bake for 10 minutes, then reduce the heat to 190ºC/375ºF/ gas mark 5 and bake for a further 20 minutes. Serve hot.

couronne

THIS BREAD – ITS FRENCH NAME MEANS "CROWN" – WAS SHAPED IN A CIRCLE SO THAT HOUSEWIVES COULD CARRY IT EASILY ON THEIR ARMS FROM THE MARKET. THE RECIPE BELOW IS A CHEAT'S VERSION OF THE BREAD, WHICH WOULD TRADITIONALLY BE MADE USING A STARTER DOUGH SUCH AS THE *BIGA* ON PAGE 12 (*SEE* VARIATION BELOW).

1 Sift the flour and salt into a large bowl and make a well in the centre. In a separate small bowl, cream the yeast and sugar with 1 tbsp of the water. Add the yeast mixture and yogurt to the well in the flour, with enough of the water to make a soft dough.

2 Tip the dough out onto a lightly floured surface and knead for 5 minutes, until it is smooth and elastic. Place it in a lightly oiled bowl, cover with a damp tea towel, and leave it to rise for 45 minutes, until it has doubled in size.

3 Knock the dough back, then tip it onto a lightly floured surface and knead for 2–3 minutes. Shape it into a 20cm (8in) round and make a hole in the centre about 12cm (5in) wide. Place the dough on a lightly greased baking sheet and make three or four diagonal cuts around the edge of the ring, which will open out like a crown. Grease the outside of a small bowl and place it in the centre of the bread to keep the shape. Leave it to prove, covered with a damp tea towel, for 30 minutes, until it has doubled in size.

4 Preheat the oven to 220°C/ 425°F/gas mark 7.

5 Remove the bowl and dust the loaf lightly with extra flour. Bake for 20–25 minutes, until it is well risen and golden and the base of the bread sounds hollow when tapped with the fingertips. Cool on a wire rack.

slow variation

A starter will enhance the flavour of the bread. Add a ½ recipe *biga* to the well in the flour along with the yeast, yogurt, and water. Continue as described above.

500G (18OZ) STRONG WHITE FLOUR

1½ TSP FINE SEA SALT

20G (¾OZ) FRESH YEAST, CRUMBLED

2 TSP CASTER SUGAR

175ML (6FL OZ) WATER AT BODY TEMPERATURE

200G (7OZ) NATURAL YOGURT

RISING: 1 hour   **PROVING:** 1 hour   **BAKING:** 20–30 minutes   **DRIED YEAST:** 2½ tsp   **MAKES:** 1 loaf

pain d'epi

THIS FRENCH BREAD WOULD TRADITIONALLY BE MADE USING A STARTER DOUGH MADE THE DAY BEFORE (*SEE* VARIATION BELOW), BUT I HAVE SHORTENED THE PROCESS. THE BREAD IS CUT SEVERAL TIMES SO THAT THE FINISHED LOAF RESEMBLES EARS OF WHEAT. THE DOUGH CAN ALSO BE USED TO MAKE SIMPLE BAGUETTES.

500G (18OZ) STRONG WHITE FLOUR

1 TBSP FINE SEA SALT

20G (¾OZ) FRESH YEAST, CRUMBLED

300ML (10FL OZ) WATER AT BODY TEMPERATURE

1 Put the flour and salt into a large bowl and make a well in the centre. Cream the yeast with 1 tbsp of the water and add it, bit by bit, to the well in the flour with the remaining water. Mix until the dough comes away from the sides of the bowl.

2 Tip the dough onto a lightly floured surface and knead it for 5 minutes, until it is smooth. Place the dough in a lightly oiled bowl, cover with a damp tea towel, and leave to rise for 1 hour, until it has doubled in size.

3 Knock the dough back, then tip it out onto a lightly floured surface and knead it for 2–3 minutes. Shape it into a baguette and place it on a lightly greased baking sheet. Using sharp scissors, make diagonal cuts halfway through the dough down each side, placing the cut flaps on alternate sides so that the loaf resembles an ear of wheat. Cover with a damp tea towel and leave to prove for 1 hour.

4 Preheat the oven to 220°C/ 425°F/gas mark 7.

5 Bake the loaf for 25–30 minutes, until it is golden and the base of the bread sounds hollow when tapped with your fingertips. Leave it to cool on a wire rack.

slow variation

You can of course use a starter. Use ½ recipe *biga* (*see* page 12), adding it to the well in the flour with the yeast and water. Continue as described above.

music-sheet bread

THIS SPECIAL SARDINIAN BREAD IS KNOWN AS *CARTA DA MUSICA,* OR "MUSIC-SHEET BREAD", BECAUSE IT SHOULD BE THIN ENOUGH FOR YOU TO READ MUSIC THROUGH IT. IT WAS ONCE A FOOD FOR THE SHEPHERDS: THEY MIGHT SOFTEN IT IN EWE'S MILK, CRUMBLE IT UP, AND DRIZZLE IT WITH HONEY FOR BREAKFAST, OR SOFTEN IT IN WATER AND FILL IT WITH VEGETABLES BEFORE BAKING IT OVER THE FIRE AS A PANCAKE FOR LUNCH.

1KG (2¼LB) FINE SEMOLINA FLOUR
(DURUM WHEAT FLOUR)

10G (¼OZ) FRESH YEAST, CRUMBLED

1 TSP COARSE SEA SALT

ABOUT 350ML (12FL OZ) WATER
AT BODY TEMPERATURE

1 Put the flour on a work surface and make a well in the middle. Dissolve the yeast and the salt separately, each in 2 tbsp of the water. Add the yeast liquid to the well with the salt water and the remaining water, and mix to a dough.

2 Knead the dough on a lightly floured surface for about 10 minutes, until it is soft, damp, and smooth. Shape it into eight balls about 8cm (3¼in) in diameter, cover with a damp tea towel, and leave to rise for about 2 hours in a dry place.

3 Preheat the oven to 200°C/400°F/gas mark 6.

4 Knock the dough back and knead it for 2–3 minutes on a lightly floured surface. Roll out the individual pieces of dough, keeping them constantly floured so they do not stick, to obtain circles of about 2–3mm (⅟₁₆–⅛in) thickness and 40cm (16in) in diameter.

5 Cook the sheets of dough, one on top of the other – all eight at the same time – in the preheated oven, and separate them only when they begin to swell.

6 At this point the bread is soft and can be used as a pancake. To make the characteristically crisp *carasau* bread, replace the sheets separately in the oven until they are dry and crunchy (about 5 minutes). Cool on a wire rack.

grissini

THESE ITALIAN BREADSTICKS CAN BE SERVED WITH STARTERS, WITH DIPS, OR AS A CANAPÉ – AND BABIES LOVE THEM. YOU CAN COAT THEM TO YOUR TASTE WITH COARSE SALT, WITH SESAME OR FENNEL SEEDS, OR WITH DRIED HERBS: TO MAKE THESE COATINGS STICK, YOU CAN BRUSH THE BREADSTICKS WITH EGG GLAZE BEFORE BAKING THEM.

I ONCE WENT TO A DINNER PARTY FOR WHICH THE FIRST-NAME INITIAL OF EVERY GUEST HAD BEEN BAKED FROM BREADSTICK DOUGH. THE INITIALS WERE THEN PRESENTED ON WHITE NAPKINS. THEY LOOKED WONDERFUL.

1 Sift the flour and salt into a large bowl and make a well in the centre. In a separate small bowl, cream the yeast and sugar with 1 tbsp of the water. Add the yeast mixture and oil to the well in the flour, together with enough of the remaining water to make a firm, sticky dough.

2 Tip the dough out onto a well-floured surface and knead it for 10 minutes, until it is smooth and elastic. Cover with a damp tea towel, and leave to rest for 10 minutes.

3 Knock back and knead the dough for a further 10 minutes on a lightly floured surface. Shape into a rectangle of about 30 x 20cm (12 x 8in) and 1.5cm (¾ in) thick. Cover it again with the tea towel and leave to rest for a further 10 minutes.

4 Preheat the oven to 200°C/ 400°F/gas mark 6. Lightly oil two baking sheets and sprinkle them with the semolina.

5 Cut the dough rectangle widthways into four equal pieces, then cut each of these pieces into 10 strips. Stretch each strip until it is about 25cm (10in) long, then roll on a flour-free surface into rounded sticks (they would slip on a floured surface). Place them well apart on the baking sheets.

6 Bake for 15–20 minutes. Transfer to a wire rack and leave to cool and become crisp.

500G (18OZ) STRONG WHITE FLOUR

2 TSP FINE SEA SALT

15G (½OZ) FRESH YEAST

½ TSP GRANULATED SUGAR

250ML (9FL OZ) WATER AT BODY TEMPERATURE

3 TBSP OLIVE OIL

2 TBSP FINE SEMOLINA

tomato and basil fougasse

THIS CLASSIC FLATTISH BREAD FROM PROVENCE IN SOUTHERN FRANCE CAN BE MADE PLAIN OR FLAVOURED — FOR INSTANCE, WITH CHEESE, SPICES, OR HERBS. I HAVE CHOSEN TO ADD INGREDIENTS HERE: SOME BASIL AND TOMATO, WHICH WORK WELL TOGETHER. YOU CAN OF COURSE LEAVE THEM OUT.

450G (1LB) STRONG WHITE FLOUR

1 TSP FINE SEA SALT

20G (¾OZ) FRESH YEAST, CRUMBLED

290ML (9FL OZ) WATER AT BODY TEMPERATURE

OLIVE OIL

115G (4OZ) SMALL CHERRY TOMATOES, CHOPPED

A HANDFUL OF FRESH BASIL LEAVES,
  ROUGHLY CHOPPED

1 Put the flour and salt into a large bowl and make a well in the centre. Cream the yeast with 1 tbsp of the water, then add it to the well in the flour with 1 tbsp of the olive oil and the remaining water. Mix until the dough comes away from the sides of the bowl.

2 Knead the dough on a lightly floured surface for about 10 minutes. Place it in a lightly oiled bowl, cover with a damp tea towel, and leave to rise for 1 hour.

3 Knock the dough back, then turn it out onto a lightly floured surface and knead for 5 minutes. Divide the dough into two equal pieces and flatten them. Sprinkle the tomatoes and basil over them and fold each piece of dough several times to incorporate the tomatoes and basil evenly.

4 Shape each piece of dough into an oblong about 28 x 15cm (11 x 6in). Using a sharp knife, make four diagonal cuts into the interior of each loaf and pull the cuts apart slightly to make a ladder effect. Place onto a lightly oiled baking sheet, cover with a damp tea towel, and leave to prove for 1 hour, until the dough has doubled in size.

5 Preheat the oven to 220°C/ 425°F/gas mark 7.

6 Drizzle each loaf with olive oil and bake for 25 minutes, until they are golden. Cool on a wire rack.

rustic walnut bread

I LOVE THIS CLASSIC WALNUT BREAD, PARTICULARLY IF IT IS SERVED WITH A STRONG CHEESE. THE COMBINATION IS VERY GOOD, BUT THE WALNUTS MUST BE FRESH. THE BREAD IS EXCELLENT FOR SANDWICHES OR FOR MOPPING UP THE JUICES FROM A GRATIN OR THE DRESSING FROM A SALAD.

600G (1LB 5OZ) STRONG WHITE FLOUR

1 TSP FINE SEA SALT

25G (1OZ) UNSALTED BUTTER, SOFTENED
    AND DICED

1 TSP FENNEL SEEDS, CRUSHED

115G (4OZ) FRESH WALNUT PIECES,
    ROUGHLY CHOPPED

15G (½OZ) FRESH YEAST, CRUMBLED

350ML (12FL OZ) WATER AT BODY TEMPERATURE

1 Sift the flour and salt into a warmed large mixing bowl. Rub in the butter until the mixture resembles bread crumbs. Stir in the fennel seeds and walnuts and make a well in the centre. Cream the fresh yeast and 2 tbsp of the water. Add this to the well in the flour and, using a wooden spoon, add as much of the remaining water as necessary to mix to a smooth ball of dough.

2 Turn the dough out onto a lightly floured work surface and knead for 10 minutes, until it is smooth. Divide the dough into two. Shape each into a round and place on an oiled baking tray. Cover with a damp tea towel and leave to rise for about 1 hour, until it has doubled in size.

3 Preheat the oven to 220°C/425°F/gas mark 7.

4 Knock the dough back, then knead it for 2–3 minutes on a lightly floured surface. Reshape, cover with the tea towel, and leave to prove for 20 minutes.

5 Slash the tops of the dough with a sharp knife and bake for 10 minutes. Reduce the temperature to 190°C/375°F/gas mark 5 and bake for a further 20 minutes, until the bread sounds hollow when tapped on the bottom with your fingertips. If the bread starts becoming too dark while cooking, cover it loosely with foil. Cool on a wire rack.

variation

You could make one loaf from this dough. It will take 1½ hours to rise, 10 minutes to prove, and 40 minutes to bake.

RISING: 1½ hours   **PROVING:** 30 minutes   **BAKING:** 5–10 minutes   **DRIED YEAST:** 2 tsp   **MAKES:** 8 breads

pitta

THIS IS THE STAPLE BREAD OF THE MIDDLE EAST, MOST COMMONLY KNOWN IN THE WEST BY ITS GREEK NAME, PITTA.
IT IS A FLATBREAD IN ESSENCE BUT IT IS ALSO A CLASSIC, WHICH IS WHY IT IS HERE IN THIS CHAPTER. IT CAN BE
EATEN WITH DIPS, USED AS A SCOOP, OR SPLIT AND USED AS A WRAP.

250G (9OZ) STRONG WHITE FLOUR

250G (9OZ) WHOLEMEAL FLOUR

1 TSP FINE SEA SALT

15G (½OZ) FRESH YEAST, CRUMBLED

½ TSP GRANULATED SUGAR

300ML (10FL OZ) WATER AT BODY TEMPERATURE

2 TBSP OLIVE OIL

1 Sift the flours and the salt into a large bowl. Some grains from the wholemeal flour will be caught in the sieve – tip them into the bowl and make a well in the centre. In a separate small bowl, cream the yeast and sugar with 1 tbsp of the water. Add the yeast mixture and olive oil to the well in the flour, with enough of the water to make a firm but soft dough.

2 Tip the dough out onto a lightly floured work surface and knead until it is smooth, supple, and elastic: about 15 minutes. It will be quite stiff at first but will stretch and become easier to work after a few minutes. Place it in a lightly oiled bowl, turn to coat evenly with oil, then cover with a damp tea towel and leave to rise for about 1½ hours, until it has doubled in size.

3 Knock the dough back, knead for 2–3 minutes, then rest, covered, for 10 minutes.

4 Divide the dough into eight pieces and shape each into a ball. Roll out on a lightly floured work surface to the characteristic pitta oval, about 22cm (9in) long and 5mm (¼in) thick. Cover with the tea towel again and leave to prove for about 20 minutes.

5 Preheat the oven to 220°C/ 425°F/gas mark 7. Dust two baking sheets lightly with flour and preheat in the oven for 5 minutes.

6 Place the ovals of bread on the two hot baking sheets and return them to the oven straight away. Bake for 5–10 minutes, until the breads puff up. Wrap in a clean, dry cloth to keep the crusts soft, because the breads can dry out fairly quickly.

BIGA: 48 hours   **RISING:** 2 hours   **PROVING:** 15 minutes   **BAKING:** 25–30 minutes   **DRIED YEAST:** 1½ tsp   **MAKES:** 1 loaf

sourdough bread

FOR ME, THIS BREAD DOUGH – INSPIRED BY ONE IN THE USA – IS THE ULTIMATE FOR FLAVOUR AND, ALTHOUGH IT DOES TAKE TIME, IT IS WELL WORTH IT. AT THE CORDON VERT COOKERY SCHOOL, WHERE I TEACH, IT HAS BEEN VOTED THE BEST BREAD, AND ONCE THE STUDENTS HAVE TRIED IT THEY ARE ALL CONVERTED. I HOPE YOU WILL BE, TOO. IT ISN'T VERY FAST, I ADMIT, BECAUSE OF THE *BIGA* (WHICH I USE INSTEAD OF THE REALLY TRADITIONAL SOURDOUGH STARTER), BUT THE INDIVIDUAL STAGES DON'T TAKE ALL THAT LONG. TRY TO FIT THESE STAGES INTO THE RHYTHM OF YOUR DAY AND THE WONDERFUL BREAD THAT RESULTS WON'T SEEM AT ALL SLOW...

10G (¼OZ) FRESH YEAST, CRUMBLED

ABOUT 225ML (8FL OZ) WATER
    AT BODY TEMPERATURE

500G (18OZ) STRONG WHITE FLOUR

½ RECIPE *BIGA* (*SEE* PAGE 12)

½ TBSP FINE SEA SALT

1 Dissolve the yeast in 50ml (2fl oz) of the water and add this and 85g (3oz) of the flour to the *biga*. Mix well. The mixture should be slack; if it is not, add a little more water. Leave for a further 24 hours.

2 The following day, add the salt and the remaining water and flour and mix together. Knead well for 10 minutes, adding more flour if necessary. Put the dough in a bowl, cover with a damp tea towel, and leave to rise in a warm place for 1 hour, until it has doubled in size.

3 Knock back and knead the dough for 2–3 minutes on a lightly floured surface. Cover with a damp tea towel and leave to rise again for a further hour.

4 Knock back for a second time. Knead for 3 minutes on a lightly floured surface, then shape into a large oval. Place on a baking tray, slash the top three times, and dust with flour. Cover and leave to prove for 15 minutes.

5 Preheat the oven to 200°C/ 400°F/gas mark 6.

6 Place a roasting tin containing a little water in the bottom of the oven – 4 tbsp should be plenty, unless it evaporates (*see* page 26 on steam). Bake the bread for 25–30 minutes, until it is golden brown and sounds hollow when tapped with your fingertips. Turn it out of the tin and cool it on a wire rack.

chocolate brioche

THIS A FAILSAFE RECIPE — ONE THAT I'VE USED FOR YEARS. PEOPLE ARE OFTEN PUT OFF BY BRIOCHE, THINKING IT DIFFICULT AND TIME-CONSUMING, BUT IT CAN BE FAST AND EASY. THE CHOCOLATE ISN'T NECESSARY BUT IS A NICE TOUCH AND IS A GREAT OCCASIONAL TREAT FOR CHILDREN.

1 Sift the flour into a large bowl with the salt and sugar and make a well in the centre. Dissolve the yeast in the water, then add it to the well in the flour with the beaten eggs and milk. Stir until you have a soft dough.

2 Turn the dough out onto a lightly floured board and knead it for 5 minutes. Add the butter a few pieces at a time; don't add the next piece until you have incorporated the first. Wrap the dough in clingfilm and refrigerate for 1 hour (or you could leave it in the fridge overnight).

3 Grease 12 small brioche pans (these have fluted edges, rather like small fairy-cake paper cases). Knock back and knead the dough on a lightly floured surface for 2–3 minutes. Divide it into 12 pieces and shape each into a smooth round. Place a square of chocolate in the centre of each and bring up the sides of the

dough. Press the edges together to seal them. Place the brioches, seam-side down, in the prepared pans, cover, and leave in a warm place to prove until they have doubled in size: about 20 minutes.

4 Preheat the oven to 200°C/400°F/gas mark 6.

5 Brush the tops of the brioches with beaten egg to glaze, then bake for 12–15 minutes. Cool slightly, then, while they are still warm, drizzle with extra melted chocolate. Serve.

variation

You could of course make plain brioche, either as one large loaf or as small loaves as above. Add a little vanilla extract to the dough first. For the large brioche, prove the dough for about 40 minutes and bake it in a 450g (1lb) loaf tin or a large brioche pan for 45 minutes. You could also bake it as a plaited loaf on a greased baking sheet.

DOUGH

250G (9OZ) STRONG WHITE FLOUR

A PINCH OF FINE SEA SALT

2 TBSP CASTER SUGAR

10G (¼OZ) FRESH YEAST, CRUMBLED

1 TBSP WATER AT BODY TEMPERATURE

3 LARGE EGGS, BEATEN

4 TBSP MILK AT BODY TEMPERATURE

115G (4OZ) UNSALTED BUTTER, DICED, AT ROOM TEMPERATURE

175G (6OZ) DARK CHOCOLATE, IN SQUARES

GLAZE AND FINISH

1 LARGE EGG, BEATEN

A LITTLE EXTRA DARK CHOCOLATE, MELTED

rolls and buns

ROLLS AND BUNS TAKE A MUCH SHORTER TIME TO RISE, PROVE, AND BAKE THAN LOAVES DO. BREAD CANNOT BE CONJURED UP IN A MINUTE; FOR THE BEST FLAVOURS AND TEXTURES, TIME IS INEVITABLY INVOLVED. BUT IF YOU DIMINISH THE SIZE OF THE DOUGH TO BE RISEN, PROVED, AND BAKED, YOU LESSEN THE TIME INVOLVED IN THE WHOLE PROCESS. ALL THE DOUGHS HERE CAN OF COURSE BE MADE INTO LOAVES, OF WHATEVER SHAPE YOU FANCY; THEY WILL JUST TAKE MUCH LONGER.

I LIKE TO THINK OF ROLLS AND BUNS AS THE FUN BREADS, WHICH ARE GREAT FOR SNACKS, PARTIES, ENTERTAINING, PICNICS, OR TRAVELLING IN THE CAR. THEY PACK EASILY, THEY CAN CONTAIN EXTRA FILLINGS, AND, BECAUSE THEY ARE

INDIVIDUAL, THEY ALWAYS HAVE THAT ELEMENT OF BEING SOMETHING SPECIAL. CHILDREN CAN HELP MAKE ROLLS AND BUNS, AND THEY LIKE TO EAT THEM, TOO. MY DAUGHTER ANTONIA LOVES THE LITTLE ROLLS I MAKE FOR HER – I THINK IT'S BECAUSE OF THE ELEMENT OF SURPRISE.

IN THIS CHAPTER WE HAVE SAVOURY AND SWEET, SOME CLASSIC, AND SOME SLIGHTLY MORE EXOTIC RECIPES. ALL HAVE BEEN DESIGNED TO FIT INTO OUR INCREASINGLY BUSY LIVES AND I HOPE THEY INSPIRE YOU TO BAKE AND CREATE EVEN MORE INTERESTING COMBINATIONS.

anchovy rolls

THESE WONDERFULLY CRISP ROLLS FEATURE IN AGRIGENTO'S WHEAT FESTIVAL CELEBRATIONS IN SICILY EVERY SPRING. THEY ARE HAND-CRAFTED BY THE WOMEN OF THE TOWN AND FRIED IN HUGE VATS OF OIL. I HAVE MODIFIED THE RECIPE A LITTLE, AND YOU CAN USE OTHER FILLINGS, SUCH AS MOZZARELLA, OLIVES AND ANCHOVIES, OR HERBS AND CHEESE. THEY ARE GREAT WITH SOUPS AND SALADS, FOR PICNICS, OR AS CANAPÉS – AND CHILDREN LOVE THEM, TOO.

DOUGH

250G (9OZ) STRONG WHITE FLOUR

2 TSP FINE SEA SALT

OLIVE OIL

10G (¼OZ) FRESH YEAST, CRUMBLED

150ML (5FL OZ) WATER AT BODY TEMPERATURE

FILLING

16 ANCHOVIES

1 In a large bowl mix the flour and salt together. Make a well in the centre and add 2 tbsp of the oil. Dissolve the yeast in a third of the water and add to the well in the flour. Using a wooden spoon, add enough of the remaining water to form a firm but damp dough.

2 Turn the dough out onto a lightly floured surface and knead for about 10 minutes. Place in a lightly oiled bowl, cover with a damp tea towel, and leave to rise for 1 hour.

3 After 1 hour, knock back the dough and knead again for 5 minutes to relax it. Cover it and leave to rest for another 5 minutes.

4 Divide the rested dough into 16 little balls. Flatten each in the palm of your hand, fill it with an anchovy, and pinch it closed into a ball, enclosing the filling. Put the little balls on a greased baking tray, seam-side down, cover, and leave to prove for 25 minutes.

5 Preheat the oven to 200°C/ 400°F/gas mark 6.

6 Bake the rolls for 12–15 minutes, until they are golden. Cool on a wire rack and eat while still warm.

RISING: 1 hour   **PROVING:** 20–30 minutes   **BAKING:** 25–35 minutes   **DRIED YEAST:** 2 tsp   **MAKES:** 6 rolls

cheese and onion crown rolls

THESE ROLLS ARE FILLING AND DELICIOUS FOR PICNICS OR FOR THE CHILDREN'S PACKED-LUNCH BOXES. THE DOUGH CAN ALSO BE BAKED AS ONE LARGE LOAF (*SEE* VARIATION BELOW).

1 TBSP OLIVE OIL

1 RED ONION, PEELED AND FINELY SLICED

55G (2OZ) UNSALTED BUTTER

100ML (3½FL OZ) MILK

15G (½OZ) FRESH YEAST, CRUMBLED

½ TSP CASTER SUGAR

2 LARGE EGGS, BEATEN

225G (8OZ) WHOLEMEAL FLOUR

1 TSP FINE SEA SALT

115G (4OZ) GRUYÈRE CHEESE, FRESHLY GRATED

1 Heat the oil in a saucepan. Add the onion and cook gently for 4–5 minutes, until it is soft but not coloured.

2 Melt the butter in the milk and, when it is up to body temperature, mix with the yeast, sugar, and eggs.

3 Put the flour and salt in a large bowl and make a well in the centre. Pour in the yeast mixture and mix to a smooth dough.

4 Tip out onto a lightly floured work surface and knead for 10 minutes. Place in a lightly oiled bowl, cover with a damp tea towel, and leave to rise for 1 hour, until the dough has doubled in size.

5 Preheat the oven to 220°C/ 425°F/gas mark 7. Lightly oil a 20cm (8in) round cake tin.

6 Knock the dough back, then turn it out onto a floured work surface and knead or chafe in the onions and three-quarters of the cheese. Divide the dough into six rolls and place in the cake tin. Leave to prove, covered with a damp tea towel, for 20–30 minutes, until they have doubled in size.

7 Bake the rolls for 20–30 minutes. Remove them from the oven, brush with a little extra milk, and sprinkle with the remaining cheese. Bake for a further 5 minutes. Leave the rolls to become cold in the tin on a wire rack before separating them.

variation
Make this dough into a free-form bread on a baking sheet – you can choose to have it round, square, oval, or long – or put it in a 450g (1lb) loaf tin. Bake it for 30–40 minutes.

cheese and potato rolls

THESE LOVELY CRUSTY ROLLS ARE A GREAT ACCOMPANIMENT TO ANY GOOD HOME-MADE SOUP. THE DOUGH CAN ALSO BE USED TO MAKE A FANTASTIC LARGE LOAF (*SEE* VARIATION BELOW).

1 Mash the potatoes with the milk and soft goat's cheese. Sift the flour into a bowl with the salt and make a well in the centre. Dissolve the yeast in 2 tbsp of the water and add to the well in the flour. Add the potato mixture and gradually mix in enough of the remaining water to make a soft dough.

2 Tip the dough out onto a lightly floured surface and knead for 10–15 minutes until it is smooth and elastic. Leave it to rise in a lightly oiled bowl, covered with a damp tea towel, for 1 hour, until it has doubled in size.

3 Preheat the oven to 220°C/ 425°F/gas mark 7.

4 Knock back the dough, then knead it again for about 2–3 minutes. Shape it into about 16 round rolls and make a cross on each roll with a sharp knife. Place them spaced apart on a greased baking sheet and lightly dust with extra flour. Cover and leave to prove for 15–20 minutes.

5 Bake the rolls for 10 minutes, then turn the oven down to 190°C/375°F/gas mark 5. Bake for a further 15 minutes, until the rolls are golden and the base sounds hollow when tapped with the fingertips. Cool on a wire rack.

variation

For a single loaf, place the dough in a greased 900g (2lb) loaf tin, then bake for 10 minutes, followed by a further 30 minutes at the lower temperature.

450G (1LB) OLD POTATOES (DÉSIRÉE, PENTLAND CROWN, OR KING EDWARD), PEELED AND FRESHLY BOILED UNTIL TENDER

150ML (5FL OZ) MILK

100G (3½OZ) SOFT GOAT'S CHEESE

675G (1½LB) STRONG WHITE FLOUR

2 TSP FINE SEA SALT

25G (1OZ) FRESH YEAST, CRUMBLED

425ML (15FL OZ) WATER AT BODY TEMPERATURE

camembert and wild mushroom rolls

THESE ROLLS ARE GREAT BATCH-BAKED IN A NEAT CIRCLE. THE WHOLE CIRCLE IS EASILY TRANSPORTED IN A PICNIC BASKET, AND EVERYBODY TEARS OFF THEIR OWN SOFT, ALREADY-FILLED ROLLS!

225G (8OZ) STRONG WHITE FLOUR

225G (8OZ) WHOLEMEAL FLOUR

1 TBSP FINE SEA SALT

55G (2OZ) UNSALTED BUTTER, SOFTENED
   AND DICED

25G (1OZ) FRESH YEAST, CRUMBLED

300ML (10FL OZ) WATER AT BODY TEMPERATURE

125G (4½OZ) WILD MUSHROOMS, SOAKED
   IF USING DRIED, ROUGHLY CHOPPED

125G (4½OZ) CAMEMBERT CHEESE, DICED

1 Put the flours and salt into a large bowl. Rub in the butter until the mixture resembles bread crumbs, then make a well in the centre. Dissolve the yeast in 2 tbsp of the water and add to the well in the flour. Mix in, adding enough of the remaining water to make a smooth dough.

2 On a lightly floured surface, knead the dough for 5 minutes until it is smooth and elastic. Place it in a lightly oiled bowl, cover with a damp tea towel, and leave to rise for 1 hour, until it has doubled in size.

3 Knock the dough back, then tip it out onto a lightly floured surface and knead for 2–3 minutes. Cut it into 12 even pieces. Roll each piece slightly and place a tsp of the mushrooms in the centre with 1 tbsp of Camembert. Carefully wrap the dough around the filling

and place the rolls, spaced apart and seam-side down, on a greased baking sheet. Cover with the tea towel and leave to prove for 20–25 minutes, until they have doubled in size.

4 Preheat the oven to 200°C/400°F/gas mark 6.

5 Dust the rolls with extra flour and bake for 10–15 minutes, until they are risen and golden. Cool on a wire rack.

variation

To make a single loaf, roll the dough out to a rectangle of about 35 x 20cm (14 x 8in). Cover with the mushrooms and Camembert and roll up like a Swiss roll, from the long side. Make several holes (with a skewer or similar) through the dough, place it on an oiled baking sheet, and bake it for 35 minutes.

brie and lardon mini-loaves

THESE MINI-LOAVES OF BREAD ARE LOVELY EATEN WHEN THEY ARE STILL SLIGHTLY WARM SO THAT THE BRIE
IS STILL SOFT, BUT ARE EQUALLY GREAT COLD FOR PICNIC BOXES.

1 Put the flour and salt into a large bowl, and rub in the butter until the mixture resembles fine bread crumbs. Cream the yeast with 2 tbsp of the milk in a small bowl. Make a well in the centre of the flour, and add the yeast liquid, eggs, and enough of the remaining milk to make a soft dough.

2 Tip the dough out onto a lightly floured surface and knead for 5 minutes, until it is smooth and elastic. Place in a lightly oiled bowl, cover with a damp tea towel, and leave to rise for 1 hour, until it has doubled in size.

3 Knock back the dough, then tip it out onto a lightly floured surface and knead for 2-3 minutes. Cut into six pieces. Roll one piece of dough at a time to a 7.5 x 10cm (3 x 4in) rectangle. Place a slice of Brie in the centre with a tsp of the bacon. Wrap the dough around the filling – folding the short ends in first, then the long ends – and then place in a greased 10 x 5.5 x 4cm (4 x 2¼ x 1½in) mini-loaf tin, seam-side down. Repeat to fill six tins.

4 Place the loaf tins on a baking sheet, cover the top with a clean tea-towel and leave to prove for 1 hour, until it has doubled in size.

5 Preheat the oven to 200°C/400°F/gas mark 6.

6 Bake the mini-loaves for 12–15 minutes, until they are golden and the base of each sounds hollow when tapped with the fingertips. Carefully loosen the loaves from the tins using a sharp knife and allow to cool slightly on a wire rack.

250G (9OZ) STRONG WHITE FLOUR

¼ TSP FINE SEA SALT

85G (3OZ) UNSALTED BUTTER, SOFTENED

25G (1OZ) FRESH YEAST, CRUMBLED

3 TBSP WARM MILK

2 LARGE EGGS, BEATEN

55G (2OZ) BRIE DE MEAUX CHEESE, CUT INTO
   6 SLICES

55G (2OZ) BACON OR PANCETTA LARDONS,
   PRE-FRIED

anchovy cloverleaf rolls

THIS IS A PROVENÇAL RECIPE AND THE ROLLS ARE LOVELY SERVED WITH A SALADE NIÇOISE. THEIR SLIGHTLY SALTY AND POWERFUL FLAVOUR MAKES THEM A GREAT ACCOMPANIMENT FOR ANY LIGHT, LEAFY SALAD.

1 Sift the flour and salt into a large bowl. Rub in the butter until the mixture resembles bread crumbs and make a well in the centre. Cream the yeast with a tbsp of the water, then add to the well in the flour, along with the eggs, brandy, and enough of the remaining water to make a smooth dough.

2 On a lightly floured work surface, knead the dough for 5 minutes, until it is smooth and elastic. Place in a lightly oiled bowl, cover with a damp tea towel, and leave to rise for 45 minutes, until it has doubled in size.

3 Knock back and then tip the dough onto a lightly floured work surface and knead in 10 of the chopped anchovies (reserve the remaining five for the topping). Divide the dough into 12 even pieces. Split each piece into three balls and place together in a

cloverleaf shape on a greased baking sheet. Cover and leave to prove for 15–20 minutes, until it has doubled in size.

4 Preheat the oven to 200°C/ 400°F/gas mark 6.

5 Brush the top of each roll with beaten egg to glaze, and sprinkle with the reserved anchovies. Bake for 12–15 minutes, until golden. Cool on a wire rack.

variation
To make one large loaf, still in the cloverleaf shape, divide the dough into three and roll into balls. Arrange in a cloverleaf shape on an oiled baking sheet and bake for 25–35 minutes.

DOUGH

500G (18OZ) STRONG WHITE FLOUR

½ TSP FINE SEA SALT

55G (2OZ) UNSALTED BUTTER, SOFTENED AND DICED

25G (1OZ) FRESH YEAST, CRUMBLED

150ML (5FL OZ) WATER AT BODY TEMPERATURE

2 LARGE EGGS, BEATEN

2 TBSP BRANDY

15 SALTED ANCHOVIES, RINSED AND FINELY CHOPPED

GLAZE

1 LARGE EGG, BEATEN

french potato bread rolls

THESE LITTLE ROLLS ARE PARTICULARLY GOOD SERVED WITH CHEESE OR AS AN ACCOMPANIMENT TO A SUBSTANTIAL
SOUP, TOPPED WITH CHEESE. THEY ARE VERY VERSATILE AND CAN ALSO BE BAKED AS A TOPPING FOR A STEW, SAY,
OR USED TO PROVIDE A BASE FOR TOPPINGS, OR THE DOUGH CAN BE BAKED INTO ONE LOAF (*SEE* VARIATION BELOW).

500G (18OZ) STRONG WHITE FLOUR

1 TSP FINE SEA SALT

225G (8OZ) WARM MASHED POTATO

15G (½OZ) FRESH YEAST, CRUMBLED

300ML (10FL OZ) MILK AND WATER IN EQUAL
    QUANTITIES, AT BODY TEMPERATURE

1 Sift the flour and salt together
into a large bowl. Rub the potato
into the flour as if rubbing in
butter, to make a smooth mixture,
and make a well in the centre.
Dissolve the yeast in a little of the
liquid and add to the well in the
flour. Using a wooden spoon, mix
in enough of the remaining liquid
to make a smooth dough.

2 Tip the dough out onto a
lightly floured surface and knead
it for 5 minutes until smooth and
elastic. Leave to rise for 40 minutes
in a lightly oiled bowl, covered
with a damp tea towel, until it
has doubled in size.

3 Preheat the oven to 220°C/
425°F/gas mark 7. Flour a
baking sheet.

4 Knead the dough once more
and divide into 12 equal pieces.
Shape into bread rolls and place
them spaced apart on the floured
baking sheet, cover lightly with a
damp tea towel, and leave to prove
for 15–20 minutes, until they have
doubled in size. Dust them lightly
with flour.

5 Bake for 12–15 minutes, until
they are risen and golden. Cool
on a wire rack.

variation

You can make this dough into one
large loaf in a 900g (2lb) loaf tin.
Bake for 25–30 minutes, perhaps
with some seeds on top.

butternut squash bread rolls

THIS IS A GOOD BREAD FOR AUTUMN, WHEN SQUASHES ARE AT THEIR BEST, AND IT CAN ALSO BE SERVED WITH A LENTIL SOUP FOR TRADITIONAL ITALIAN NEW YEAR'S EVE FARE. THE LENTILS SIGNIFY THAT THE NEW YEAR WILL BRING MONEY.

1 Put half of the flour on the work surface and make a well in the centre. Heat the milk until just warm, then cream the yeast in a little of it. Add the yeast liquid to the well in the flour, along with the remaining milk, and mix to a dough.

2 Knead the dough for 10 minutes, until it is smooth. Put it into an oiled bowl, cover with a damp tea towel, and leave to rise for 1 hour.

3 Meanwhile, preheat the oven to 200°C/400°F/gas mark 6, and oil a baking sheet. Bake the squash for 20 minutes, until it is soft. Purée the squash with a masher, then mix in the raisins. Allow it to cool before adding it to the dough.

4 Knock the dough back. Add the squash and raisins to the dough with the remaining flour on a lightly floured work surface, and knead well for 10 minutes. Return to the oiled bowl, cover with a damp tea towel, and leave to rise for a further hour.

5 Preheat the oven to 200°C/400°F/gas mark 6. Lightly butter a baking tray.

6 Divide the dough into five pieces. Form each into a slightly flat circle and arrange the circles about 5–8cm (2–3in) apart on the buttered baking tray. Cover with the tea towel and leave to prove for a further 10 minutes.

7 Bake the rolls for 25 minutes, during which time they will join up into a flat loaf. Remove from the oven and cool a little on a wire rack before breaking into rolls and then pieces.

300G 10½OZ) STRONG WHITE FLOUR

100ML (3½FL OZ) FULL-FAT MILK

10G (¼OZ) FRESH YEAST, CRUMBLED

250G (9OZ) BUTTERNUT SQUASH, PEELED, DESEEDED, AND FINELY DICED

75G (2¾OZ) RAISINS, SOAKED IN WARM WATER FOR 20 MINUTES AND SQUEEZED DRY

OLIVE OIL

UNSALTED BUTTER

BIGA: 8–12 hours   RISING: 3 hours   PROVING: 15 minutes   BAKING: 15–20 minutes   DRIED YEAST: ½ tsp (*biga*) and 2 tsp (dough)

MAKES: 12 rolls

slipper bread rolls

CIABATTA'S ORIGINS LIE IN EMILIA-ROMAGNA, THE GASTRONOMIC CENTRE OF ITALY. IT IS A RECIPE THAT I AM CONSTANTLY HONING, BUT I AM NOW TRULY HAPPY WITH THE RESULTS. IF YOU DO THE VARIOUS STAGES AT TIMES CONVENIENT TO YOU, IT WON'T TAKE VERY LONG.

CIABATTA *BIGA*

250G (9OZ) STRONG WHITE FLOUR

5G (⅛OZ) FRESH YEAST, CRUMBLED

150ML (5FL OZ) WATER AT BODY TEMPERATURE

CIABATTA DOUGH

300ML (10FL OZ) WATER AT BODY TEMPERATURE

15G (½OZ) FRESH YEAST, CRUMBLED

500G (18OZ) STRONG WHITE FLOUR

2 TSP FINE SEA SALT

4 TBSP OLIVE OIL

1 Start with the *biga*. Put the flour in a large bowl and make a well in the centre. Dissolve the yeast in 1 tbsp of the water and add it to the well with enough of the remaining water to mix it to a slack dough.

2 Knead it on a work surface for 2 minutes, return it to the bowl, cover with a damp tea towel, and leave at room temperature for 8–12 hours. It will rise and then fall.

3 The next day, put the water for the ciabatta in a jug or bowl and crumble in the yeast. Mix well, then add it to the *biga*. Stir and squeeze with your fingers to make a thick, smooth dough. Work in half the flour to make a very sticky dough and beat it with your hands for 5 minutes, until it is well stretched and elastic. Cover the bowl with a damp tea towel and leave the dough to rise in a warm place until it has doubled in size: about 2 hours.

4 Add the salt and oil to the dough, then gradually work in the rest of the flour to make a soft, sticky dough. Carry on kneading until it is smooth and very elastic, cover with a damp tea towel, and leave to rise in a warm place until it has doubled in size: about 1 hour.

5 Meanwhile, preheat the oven to 200°C/400°F/gas mark 6, and gently warm a baking sheet.

6 Carefully tip the dough onto a well-floured work surface. Using a well-floured bread scraper or palette knife, divide it into 12 pieces. Don't make them uniform: odd shapes add charm. Dust with flour, then cover with a damp tea towel and leave to prove for 15 minutes.

7 Knock the rolls back slightly – dimpling them with your thumb – then bake for 15–20 minutes, until they are golden brown and crisp.

variation

To make two slipper-shaped loaves, prove the dough for 30 minutes and then bake for 25–30 minutes.

BIGA: 24 hours   **RISING:** 2 hours   **PROVING:** 30 minutes   **BAKING:** 20 minutes   **DRIED YEAST:** ½ tsp (*biga*) and 1 tsp (dough)

MAKES: 12 rolls

semolina bread rolls

THESE ROLLS ARE FROM PUGLIA IN SOUTHERN ITALY AND ARE IDEAL FOR BREAKFAST. SEMOLINA IMPARTS COLOUR AND A SLIGHTLY GRAINY TEXTURE AND CRUST. FLAVOUR THE DOUGH WITH A HANDFUL OF CHOPPED FRESH HERBS (OR A SPRINKLING OF DRIED) IF YOU WANT TO.

1 Place the flour, semolina, and black pepper on a work surface, pile into a mound, and make a well in the centre. Dissolve the yeast in 2 tbsp of the water, then add this and the *biga* to the well in the flour, along with the remaining water. Mix with your hands until all the ingredients are well combined, which will take about 5 minutes.

2 Add the fine salt and knead the dough for 10 minutes, until it is smooth and elastic. Do the stretch test to check that the dough is ready (*see* page 18). Place the dough in a large, lightly oiled bowl, cover with a damp tea towel, and leave in a warm place until it has doubled in size: approximately 1½ hours.

3 Knock back the dough, knead for 2–3 minutes on a lightly floured surface, then cover and leave to rise again for 30 minutes. This second rising will give the dough more strength.

4 Tip the dough onto a lightly floured surface and cut into 12 pieces, using a dough scraper or sharp knife. Shape into balls, place on a lightly oiled baking tray, and leave to prove for half an hour.

5 Preheat the oven to 200°C/ 400°F/gas mark 6.

6 Using a sharp knife, cut a cross on top of each roll, then sprinkle liberally with coarse salt. Bake in the preheated oven for 20 minutes, opening the oven door slightly for the last 5 minutes to make the rolls crisper. Cool a little on a wire rack and eat warm.

375G (13OZ) STRONG WHITE FLOUR

275G (10OZ) FINE SEMOLINA

2 TSP COARSELY GROUND BLACK PEPPER

10G (¼OZ) FRESH YEAST, CRUMBLED

375ML (13 FL OZ) WATER AT BODY TEMPERATURE

1 RECIPE *BIGA* (*SEE* PAGE 12)

15G (½OZ) FINE SEA SALT

OLIVE OIL

2 TBSP COARSE SEA SALT

hot cross buns

THESE BUNS ARE TRADITIONAL AT EASTER BUT ARE GREAT AT ANY TIME OF YEAR, ESPECIALLY IN WINTER WHEN ALL THEIR SPICES CONJURE UP IMAGES OF COMFORT AND WARM TEAS IN FRONT OF THE FIRE. THEY ARE DELICIOUS SPLIT AND TOASTED, WITH LOADS OF BUTTER – AND JAM, IF YOU WISH.

1 Sift the flour into a large bowl, add the butter, and rub it in with your fingertips until the mixture resembles fine bread crumbs. Stir in the sugar, salt, and spices and make a well in the centre. Blend the yeast with 2 tbsp of the milk in a small bowl and add to the well in the flour, together with the egg and enough of the remaining milk to form a smooth dough.

2 Knead the dough for 5 minutes on a lightly floured work surface, until it is smooth and elastic. Gradually incorporate the raisins, sultanas, and candied peel. Place the dough in a lightly oiled bowl, cover with a damp tea towel, and leave to rise for 1 hour, until it has doubled in size.

3 Knock back the dough, then tip it out onto a lightly floured surface and knead for 2–3 minutes.

Cut it into 12 even pieces and shape into balls. Place on a greased baking sheet, spaced well apart. Cover with a damp tea towel and leave to prove for an hour, until it has doubled in size.

4 Preheat the oven to 200°C/ 400°F/gas mark 6.

5 Mix the water, flour, and egg in a bowl to make a paste for the crosses. Pour into a small plastic bag and tie a knot in the top. Snip the corner of the bag. Pipe crosses onto each bun.

6 Bake the buns for 15 minutes, until they are golden. While they are still warm, brush them with golden syrup. Cool on a wire rack.

DOUGH

450G (1LB) STRONG WHITE FLOUR

85G (3OZ) UNSALTED BUTTER, SOFTENED AND DICED

85G (3OZ) SOFT LIGHT BROWN SUGAR

1 TSP SALT

1 TSP MIXED SPICE

¼ TSP FRESHLY GRATED NUTMEG

½ TSP GROUND CINNAMON

20G (¾OZ) FRESH YEAST, CRUMBLED

250ML (9FL OZ) MILK AT BODY TEMPERATURE

1 LARGE EGG, BEATEN

115G (4OZ) RAISINS

85G (3OZ) SULTANAS

55G (2OZ) CANDIED LEMON PEEL, FINELY CHOPPED

CROSSES

100ML (3½FL OZ) WATER

100G (3½OZ) PLAIN FLOUR

1 MEDIUM EGG

GLAZE

2 TBSP GOLDEN SYRUP

banana, maple syrup, and pecan rolls

THESE LITTLE ROLLS ARE MY FRIEND BRIDGET'S VARIATION ON THE BRITISH "TOASTED TEACAKES". THEY ARE GREAT SERVED AT TEATIME AND ARE LOVELY TOASTED WITH BUTTER AND AN EXTRA DRIZZLE OF MAPLE SYRUP.

500G (18OZ) STRONG WHITE FLOUR

1 TSP FINE SEA SALT

15G (½OZ) FRESH YEAST, CRUMBLED

425ML (15FL OZ) WATER AT BODY TEMPERATURE

2 TBSP MAPLE SYRUP

2 BANANAS, PEELED AND CHOPPED

115G (4OZ) SHELLED PECAN NUTS, TOASTED AND ROUGHLY CHOPPED

1 Sift the flour and salt into a large bowl and make a well in the centre. Cream the yeast with 1 tbsp of the water and put into the well in the flour along with most of the maple syrup. Mix, gradually adding enough of the remaining water to make a soft, smooth dough.

2 Tip the dough out onto a lightly floured surface and knead for 10–15 minutes, until it is smooth and elastic. Place in a lightly oiled bowl, cover with a damp tea towel, and leave to rise for 1 hour, until it has doubled in size.

3 Knock back and knead the dough on a lightly floured surface for 2–3 minutes, then knead or chafe to incorporate the bananas and pecans. Divide the dough into 10 balls and place in a batch, nestling together, on an oiled

baking sheet. Leave to prove, covered with a damp tea towel, for 30 minutes, until they have doubled in size. Preheat the oven to 200°C/400°F/gas mark 6.

4 Bake the rolls for 20–25 minutes, until they have risen and are golden. While they are still warm, drizzle the tops with the remaining maple syrup. Leave to cool on a wire rack before separating them.

variation

Shape the dough into one loaf – preferably free-form – and bake for about 35–40 minutes.

lavender and honey knots

THESE PRETTY BREAD ROLLS ARE LOVELY SERVED AT TEATIME WITH BUTTER AND HONEY. THEY CAN ALSO EASILY

BE MADE INTO A LOAF (*SEE* VARIATION BELOW).

1 Preheat the oven to 220°C/ 425°F/gas mark 7.

2 Put half the white and wholemeal flours into a large bowl and make a well in the centre. Dissolve the yeast in 150ml (5fl oz) of the water and pour into the well in the flour. Mix well for 5 minutes, then leave to rest for 30 minutes, covered with a damp tea towel.

3 Add the remaining flours and water and the salt, honey, and lavender to the dough and knead it well on a lightly floured surface for 5 minutes, until it is smooth and elastic. Leave to rest for 30 minutes in a lightly oiled bowl, covered with a damp tea towel, until it has doubled in size.

4 Knock the dough back and knead for 2–3 minutes on a lightly floured surface. Divide the dough into 12 equal pieces. Working with one piece at a time, roll the dough backward and forward until it is

about 30–40cm (12–16in) in length. Tie each strip into a loose knot and place on a greased baking sheet. Do the same with all the other pieces of dough. Mix the egg and honey together for the glaze and brush it onto each roll. Cover and leave to prove for 30–40 minutes.

5 Bake for 15–20 minutes, until the knots are risen and golden and the base of the bread sounds hollow when tapped with the fingertips. Leave them to cool on a wire rack.

variation

To make one free-form loaf, mix half of the flours, all the yeast, and half the water and leave to rest for 4 hours. Add the remaining ingredients, knead, then leave to rest for a further half-hour. Knock back, shape into a ball with a circle scored on the top, and leave to prove for an hour. Bake for 30 minutes.

DOUGH

250G (9OZ) STRONG WHITE FLOUR

250G (9OZ) WHOLEMEAL FLOUR

25G (1OZ) FRESH YEAST, CRUMBLED

300ML (10FL OZ) WATER AT BODY TEMPERATURE

1 TBSP FINE SEA SALT

75ML (2½FL OZ) RUNNY HONEY

1 TBSP CULINARY LAVENDER FLOWERS

GLAZE

1 LARGE EGG, BEATEN

1 TBSP RUNNY HONEY

pizzas and flatbreads

ALL BREADS WOULD HAVE BEEN FLAT AT ONE TIME, BEFORE THE POWER OF LEAVENING WAS DISCOVERED (THROUGH AIRBORNE YEASTS, STILL THE BASIS OF THE MOST TRADITIONAL SOURDOUGH BREADS) AND BEFORE OVENS WERE COMMONLY AVAILABLE. BASIC MIXTURES OF GRAIN AND WATER WOULD HAVE BEEN BAKED ON A FLAT SURFACE – A STONE BESIDE A FIRE OR A GIRDLE HUNG ABOVE A FIRE. THE OATCAKE ON PAGE 163 IS A CLASSIC EXAMPLE OF AN OLD YEAST-FREE "FLATBREAD". MANY INTERNATIONAL BREADS ARE STILL FLAT IN ESSENCE, ALTHOUGH THEY MIGHT NOW USE LEAVENS SUCH AS YEAST: THE MIDDLE EASTERN PITTA, FOR INSTANCE (*SEE* PAGE 47) AND THE INDIAN *NAAN*.

THE PIZZA STARTED OFF AS A SIMPLE BREAD IN MUCH THE SAME WAY, BEFORE THE CANNY NEAPOLITANS DECIDED TO ADD TOPPINGS. PIZZA IS NOW A WORLDWIDE PHENOMENON, BUT THERE IS NOTHING QUITE LIKE A HOME-MADE ONE. THERE ARE FOUR PIZZA DOUGHS HERE – ONE VERY QUICK TO MAKE, THE OTHERS SLOWER. ALL ARE DELICIOUS,

AND THEY ARE SO VARIABLE: YOU CAN MAKE LARGE, CIRCULAR PIZZAS TO SHARE, PIZZA "SWISS ROLLS", *CALZONI*
(FOLDED PIZZAS), OR TINY PIZZA CANAPÉS TO SERVE AT A PARTY.

TO SAVE ON TIME, YOU COULD DO AS I DO: MAKE DOUBLE THE QUANTITY OF DOUGH, AND FREEZE HALF. THERE
IS ABSOLUTELY NOTHING WRONG WITH FREEZING DOUGH AND, IN FACT, ONCE OUT OF THE FREEZER AND DEFROSTING, IT
IS RISING AT THE SAME TIME. I TAKE MY DOUGH OUT FIRST THING IN THE MORNING AND WHEN I COME HOME AT NIGHT
IT IS READY TO BAKE — SO, IN ESSENCE, THERE IS NO TIME INVOLVED AT ALL!

KIDS LOVE FLATBREADS AND PIZZAS, SO THIS IS QUITE A CHILD-FRIENDLY CHAPTER. THEY COULD HELP TMAKE
THE DOUGH, AS WELL AS CHOOSE THEIR OWN TOPPINGS FOR PIZZAS. EVEN DIET-CONSCIOUS PEOPLE CAN TAKE TO
THESE BREADS — THEY ARE "SKINNY", WITH ALL THE TASTE BUT WITH MUCH LESS BREAD.

semolina pizza dough

THIS IS A CLASSIC, TENDER NEAPOLITAN DOUGH, MADE WITH HARD-WHEAT SEMOLINA. IT HAS TAKEN ME A LONG TIME TO PERFECT THIS RECIPE AND THE RESULT IS A MUCH CRISPER CRUST THAN MANY RECIPES GIVE. IF YOU HAVE THE TIME, THIS DOUGH IS EVEN BETTER IF ALLOWED TO RISE FOR 4–6 HOURS.

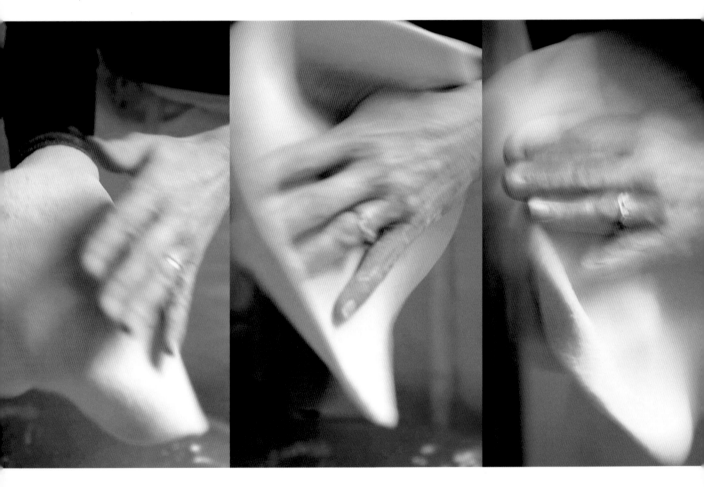

1 Combine the flours and salt in a large bowl and make a well in the centre. Dissolve the yeast in 2 tbsp of the water. Gradually add the yeast mixture to the well in the dough, along with enough of the remaining water to create a soft pliable dough.

2 Knead the dough on a lightly floured surface for 10 minutes, until it is smooth and elastic. Shape the dough into a ball, cover with a damp tea towel, and leave it to rise for 1 hour or until it has doubled in size.

3 Knock back the dough and divide it into two pieces. Roll these pieces into circles and place them on a floured work surface. Cover with a damp tea towel and leave to prove for 30 minutes.

4 Knock the dough back, then roll it out and shape accordingly (*see* individual recipes).

150G (5½OZ) FINE SEMOLINA

100G (3½OZ) ITALIAN "00" PLAIN FLOUR

1 TSP FINE SEA SALT

10G (¼OZ) FRESH YEAST, CRUMBLED

50ML (2FL OZ) WATER AT BODY TEMPERATURE

RISING: 1 hour   **PROVING:** 1 hour   **BAKING:** *see* individual recipes   **DRIED YEAST:** 1 tsp   **MAKES:** enough for 2 x 25 cm (10in) pizzas

quick-rise pizza dough

THE SEMOLINA PIZZA DOUGH IS WONDERFUL, BUT IT TAKES UP TO 6 HOURS TO RISE (BUT CAN BE DONE IN 1 HOUR; *SEE* PAGE 75). THIS ONE, HOWEVER, TAKES MUCH LESS TIME AND IS STILL VERY GOOD, GIVING A CRISP, TASTY RESULT.

250G (9OZ) STRONG WHITE FLOUR

1 TSP FINE SEA SALT

10G (¼OZ) FRESH YEAST, CRUMBLED

50ML (2FL OZ) WATER AT BODY TEMPERATURE

1 Mix the flour and salt in a large bowl and make a well in the centre. Dissolve the yeast in the water, then add it to the well in the flour and mix well to form a raggy dough.

2 Tip the dough out onto a lightly floured surface and knead for 10 minutes. Shape it into a ball, place in an oiled bowl, cover with a damp tea towel, and leave to rise for 1 hour.

3 Knock back the dough and knead it on a lightly floured surface for another 10 minutes. Return the dough to the bowl, cover again, and leave to prove for a further hour.

4 Knock the dough back and shape it accordingly (*see* individual recipes).

slow variation

A classic dough for making Neapolitan-style pizza uses exactly the same ingredients as this recipe, but it just needs longer for kneading, rising, and proving. The taste and texture are infinitely superior.

Knead for a further 10 minutes until the dough is strong, soft as silk, and very elastic. Shape it into a ball and leave it on the lightly floured surface – covered with a clean bowl – for 4 hours, until it has doubled in size.

Knock the dough back and divide it in half. Cover the pieces again and leave them to prove for 2 hours, until they have doubled in size.

Knock back and shape accordingly (*see* individual recipes).

red onion and goat's cheese pizza tart

THIS IS MY VARIATION OF THE TRADITIONAL FRENCH PIZZA-TYPE TART, *PISSALADIÈRE*. IT IS OFTEN MADE USING PASTRY BUT IS EQUALLY DELICIOUS WITH A BREAD BASE. IT MAKES A GREAT VEGETARIAN LIGHT LUNCH WITH SALAD.

1 Mix the flour and salt into a large bowl and make a well in the centre. Cream the yeast with 1 tbsp of the water and add it to the well in the flour with the olive oil and remaining water. Mix until the dough comes away from the sides of the bowl.

2 Tip the dough onto a lightly floured surface and knead for 5 minutes, until it is smooth. Place it in a lightly oiled bowl, cover with a damp tea towel, and leave to rise for 1 hour, until it has doubled in size.

3 Meanwhile, heat the oil for the topping in a frying pan. Add the onion and fry gently for 15 minutes, until it has softened. Stir in the sugar and garlic. Fry for 5 more minutes, until the onions are beginning to caramelize, then stir in the thyme. Set aside to cool slightly.

4 Knock the dough back, then tip it out onto a lightly floured surface and knead for 5 minutes, until it is smooth and elastic. Roll it out to a circle of about 30cm (12in) in diameter. Spoon the onions evenly over the dough base, leaving a narrow border of dough around the edges. Scatter the goat's cheese over it and season with salt and pepper. Cover loosely and leave to prove for 30 minutes.

5 Preheat the oven to 220°C/425°F/gas mark 7.

6 Bake the tart for 12–15 minutes, until the dough looks golden. Cool a little on a wire rack, and eat hot, warm, or cold.

DOUGH

250G (9OZ) STRONG WHITE FLOUR

½ TSP FINE SEA SALT

15G (½OZ) FRESH YEAST, CRUMBLED

150ML (5FL OZ) WATER AT BODY TEMPERATURE

2 TBSP OLIVE OIL

TOPPING

3 TBSP OLIVE OIL

3 MEDIUM RED ONIONS, PEELED AND THINLY SLICED

1 TSP CASTER SUGAR

2 GARLIC CLOVES, PEELED AND CRUSHED

1 TBSP ROUGHLY CHOPPED FRESH THYME

150G (5½OZ) GOAT'S CHEESE, CRUMBLED

SEA SALT AND FRESHLY GROUND BLACK PEPPER

pizza tartlets

THROUGHOUT ITALY, THERE ARE AS MANY TOPPINGS FOR PIZZA AS THERE ARE SAUCES FOR PASTA. JUST ABOUT ANY COMBINATION OF INGREDIENTS CAN BE TRANSFORMED INTO A CRISPY BAKED DELICACY. PIZZA TARTLETS ARE A COMMON FESTIVE FOOD AMONG SICILIANS.

1 RECIPE QUICK-RISE PIZZA DOUGH (*SEE* PAGE 76), OR OTHER OF CHOICE

OLIVE OIL

SEA SALT AND FRESHLY GROUND BLACK PEPPER

TOPPING 1

1 SMALL RED PEPPER

1 SMALL YELLOW PEPPER

200G (7OZ) MIXED MUSHROOMS, I.E. PORCINI OR FIELD, FINELY CHOPPED

100G (3½OZ) FONTINA CHEESE, SHAVED

TOPPING 2

4 SMALL COURGETTES

4 RIPE PLUM TOMATOES, HALVED

1 TSP FINELY CHOPPED FRESH MINT

100G (3½OZ) SMOKED MOZZARELLA OR SCAMORZA CHEESE, CUT INTO 1CM (½IN) CUBES

TOPPING 3

1 SMALL AUBERGINE, PEELED AND CUT INTO 1CM (½IN) CUBES

1 X 100G CAN TUNA IN BRINE, DRAINED

100G (3½OZ) BUFFALO MOZZARELLA, CUT INTO 1CM (½IN) CUBES

12 BLACK OLIVES, STONED AND CHOPPED

TOPPING 4

2 MEDIUM ONIONS, PEELED AND FINELY SLICED

ABOUT 75ML (2½FL OZ) WATER

A HANDFUL OF ROCKET LEAVES, STEMS REMOVED

½ GARLIC CLOVE, PEELED AND CRUSHED

½ TSP PAPRIKA

1 Preheat the oven to 200°C/ 400°F/gas mark 6.

2 Roast the peppers for Topping 1 for 20 minutes. Leave to cool, then skin and deseed, and cut into thin strips. Set aside. Keep the oven on, and turn it up to 220°C/ 425°F/gas mark 7.

3 Heat about 2 tbsp of the oil in a frying pan over medium heat and sauté the aubergine for Topping 3 for 7–9 minutes, stirring constantly. Season with salt and pepper and set aside. Heat a little more oil in the same pan and sauté the mushrooms for Topping 1 for 4 minutes. Season with salt and pepper. Set aside.

4 Add a little more oil to the same pan and sauté the onion for Topping 4. Add the water and cook for 8 minutes or until the onion is coarsely wilted.

5 Parboil the courgette for Topping 2 in salted water for 5 minutes. Lift out with a slotted spoon, cut into thin slices, and set aside. Parboil the rocket for Topping 4 in the same water for 2 minutes. Drain and squeeze dry.

6 Heat a little more olive oil in the frying pan over a high heat and sauté the tomatoes for Topping 2 for 8 minutes, stirring constantly. Transfer to a bowl, toss with the mint, and set aside.

7 Heat 1 tbsp of oil in a frying pan, add the garlic and rocket for Topping 4, and toss well for 1 minute. Season with salt and pepper, and set aside.

8 Oil 12 x 7.5cm (3in) round individual tart pans.

9 Put the knocked-back dough on a lightly floured surface and knead for 2–3 minutes. Roll into

a large rectangle about 3mm (⅛in) thick. Cut into 12 x 7.5cm (3in) circles and arrange in the tart pans, pressing the edges against the sides. Cover the surface of each tart with parchment paper and weigh it down with baking beans.

10 Bake the tart cases for 10 minutes. Remove from the oven and remove the beans and paper.

11 Top three of the little tarts with peppers, mushrooms, and fontina; three with courgette, tomato, mint, and mozzarella; three with aubergine, tuna, mozzarella, and olives; and three with onion, rocket, garlic, and paprika.

12 Return to the oven and bake for 10 minutes. Remove from the tart pans and serve immediately.

little pizzas

PIZZETTE ARE THE PERFECT APPETIZER PIZZAS. FOR A CHILDREN'S PARTY, OFFER THEM WITH A VARIETY OF TOPPINGS, SUCH AS ROASTED RED AND YELLOW PEPPERS WITH PINE NUTS, OR A CLASSIC TOMATO SAUCE WITH BASIL AND MOZZARELLA. EXPERIMENT WITH THE TOPPINGS TO CREATE A VARIETY OF GORGEOUS FLAVOURS.

DOUGH

1 RECIPE QUICK-RISE PIZZA DOUGH (*SEE* PAGE 76), OR OTHER OF CHOICE

2 TSP FINELY GRATED UNWAXED LEMON ZEST

TOPPING

150G (5½OZ) TOMATOES, CUT INTO 2.5CM (1IN) CHUNKS

1 RED ONION, PEELED AND THINLY SLICED

3 TBSP OLIVE OIL

1 TBSP CAPERS, RINSED AND DRAINED

1 TBSP FINELY CHOPPED FRESH FLAT-LEAF PARSLEY

1 TBSP EXTRA VIRGIN OLIVE OIL

1 Preheat the oven to 200°C/400°F/gas mark 6 for at least 30 minutes with a pizza stone inside.

2 Make the dough and knead the lemon zest into it as you knock it back. Divide the dough into 12 pieces and form each piece into a ball. Place on a lightly floured work surface, cover with a damp tea towel, and leave to prove for 10 minutes.

3 Knock back the dough, then pat and stretch each ball to a thickness of 1cm (½in), leaving the outer edge slightly thicker. Each round will be about 10cm (4in) in diameter.

4 Place each round on a floured double pizza paddle or baking sheet. Lightly brush the rounds with olive oil. Drop the tomato and onion over the tops of the rounds. Drizzle with oil, and slide the pizzas onto the pizza stone.

5 Bake for 4–5 minutes or until the edges are golden brown. Remove from the oven, and sprinkle with capers, parsley, and the extra virgin olive oil. Serve immediately.

mini fried potato pizzas

CULLURELLI ARE SMALL FRIED PIZZAS ASSOCIATED WITH THE TRADITIONAL MEATLESS MEALS SERVED ON CHRISTMAS EVE IN ITALY. IN SOVERATO, A SMALL COASTAL VILLAGE ON THE CALABRIAN INSTEP OF THE ITALIAN BOOT, THESE DELICIOUS PIZZAS ARE MADE OUTDOORS IN HUGE COMMUNITY FRYING PANS PLACED OVER WOOD-BURNING FIRES.

1 Put the flour and salt in a large bowl, mix, and make a well in the centre. Dissolve the yeast in some of the water. Add 1 tbsp of the oil and the potato to the well, along with the dissolved yeast, and mix with enough of the remaining water to make a damp dough.

2 Turn the dough out of the bowl and knead well on a lightly floured work surface for about 10 minutes, until the mixture is smooth and elastic. Return to a clean bowl, cover with a clean tea towel, and leave to rise for 1 hour.

3 Knock back the dough and knead again on a lightly floured surface for 5 minutes. Allow the dough to relax for 5 minutes before pinching off walnut-sized pieces and rolling them into 5cm (2in) rounds. Put the rounds on a lightly floured surface and continue rolling small pieces until all the dough has been used up.

4 Heat 5cm (2in) olive oil in a heavy frying pan. Fry the pizza rounds three or four at a time until they are golden on both sides. Remove them with a slotted spoon, drain on kitchen paper, and serve immediately.

300G (10½OZ) STRONG WHITE FLOUR

1½ TSP FINE SEA SALT

10G (¼OZ) FRESH YEAST, CRUMBLED

100ML (3½FL OZ) WATER AT BODY TEMPERATURE

OLIVE OIL

1 MEDIUM OLD POTATO, BOILED, PEELED AND PUT
    THROUGH A MOULI OR SIEVE

fried stuffed pizzas

LITTLE FRIED SNACKS LIKE THESE ARE COMMON ON THE STREETS OF NAPLES. THEY MAKE A REALLY SATISFYING LUNCH AND, BECAUSE THEY ARE SEALED PARCELS, THEY ARE EMINENTLY PORTABLE.

1 In a frying pan, heat the olive oil on medium and sauté the onion until the edges are golden: about 4–5 minutes. Add the spinach and cook for 5 minutes, until it is wilted. Remove from the heat and cool. Stir in the cheeses, mix well, and season with salt and pepper to taste. Set aside.

2 Knead the knocked-back dough on a lightly floured surface for 2–3 minutes. Divide it into 12 pieces. Pat and stretch each piece to a thickness of about 5mm (¼in) and a diameter of about 13cm (5in). Divide the filling evenly between the rounds, leaving a 1cm (½in) rim. Fold each round in half, rolling the bottom edge over the top and pinching to seal firmly.

3 In a large frying pan, heat 5cm (2in) of olive oil for frying. Fry the *calzoni* for 2–3 minutes on each side or until the edges are golden brown. Drain well on kitchen paper and serve at once.

DOUGH

1 RECIPE QUICK-RISE PIZZA DOUGH (*SEE* PAGE 76), OR OTHER OF CHOICE

OLIVE OIL

FILLING

3 TBSP OLIVE OIL

1 SMALL ONION, PEELED AND DICED

300G (10½OZ) FRESH SPINACH, WASHED, TOUGH STEMS REMOVED

125G (4½OZ) RICOTTA CHEESE

85G (3OZ) PARMESAN, FRESHLY GRATED

55G (2OZ) GORGONZOLA CHEESE, CRUMBLED

SEA SALT AND FRESHLY GROUND PEPPER

sicilian stuffed pizza

SFINCIONE (AS THIS IS KNOWN IN ITALY) IS A POPULAR SICILIAN STUFFED PIZZA. THIS VERSION, WITH ITS SIMPLE AND HEARTY INGREDIENTS, QUALIFIES AS THE ULTIMATE COMFORT FOOD.

DOUGH

1 RECIPE QUICK-RISE PIZZA DOUGH (*SEE* PAGE 76), OR OTHER OF CHOICE

FILLING

1 MEDIUM AUBERGINE, PEELED AND DICED

FINE SEA SALT AND FRESHLY GROUND BLACK PEPPER

OLIVE OIL

1 SMALL ONION, PEELED AND FINELY CHOPPED

150G (5½OZ) MINCED PORK

1 GARLIC CLOVE, PEELED AND FINELY CHOPPED

7 FRESH TOMATOES, SEEDED AND CHOPPED

1 TBSP TOMATO PURÉE

2 PINCHES DRIED OREGANO

1 Spread the aubergine pieces out in one layer on a baking sheet. Sprinkle with salt and weigh it down with another baking sheet. Leave for about 10 minutes. Rinse, drain, and pat the aubergine dice dry with kitchen paper.

2 Heat 3 tbsp of oil in a medium frying pan over a medium heat and cook the onion until it is softened but not brown: about 2 minutes. Add the pork and cook until it is slightly browned: about 4–5 minutes. Add the aubergine and garlic and cook for a further 4–5 minutes, stirring frequently. Add the tomatoes, tomato purée, oregano, and some salt and pepper and cook until the mixture has thickened: another 20 minutes. Adjust the seasoning to taste and set aside.

3 Preheat the oven to 200°C/ 400°F/gas mark 6 for at least 30 minutes with a pizza stone inside (if you have one).

4 Knead the knocked-back dough on a lightly floured surface for 2–3 minutes, then divide it into six pieces. Pat then stretch the pieces to a thickness of 1cm (½in) and a diameter of about 25cm (10in). Place three of the rounds on a flour-dusted pizza paddle or a baking sheet. Spread some of the filling in the centre of each pizza, leaving a 1cm (½in) rim. Top with another round of dough, and pinch the edges to seal. With a sharp knife, make three slashes on the top, and brush with olive oil.

5 Slide the three pizzas onto the pizza stone and bake for 20 minutes or until the edges are golden brown. Remove from the oven, cut in half, and serve at once.

spinach and olive stuffed pizza

THIS PIZZA-BREAD DOUGH ENCLOSES A FILLING OF SPINACH AND OLIVES, SEASONED WITH GARLIC AND CHILLI, LIKE A LARGE PARCEL. IT IS A DELICIOUS LUNCH OR SUPPER MEAL SERVED WITH A SALAD, OR A GREAT PICNIC BREAD. I FIRST ENCOUNTERED THIS RECIPE AT NAPLES AIRPORT AND IT WAS THE FIRST TIME I HAD SEEN SPINACH IN A BREAD CASING.

1 To prepare the filling, peel and slice the onion and crush the garlic and red chilli. Wash the spinach well and chop roughly, discarding any coarse stalks. Heat the oil in a saucepan, add the onion, and cook it for about 5 minutes, until it is soft. Add the garlic and chilli and cook for 1 minute. Add the spinach and olives and cook until the spinach just begins to wilt. Remove from the heat and stir in the cheese. Season with salt and pepper.

2 When the dough has risen, knock it back, then turn it onto a lightly floured surface and knead for 2–3 minutes. Divide it in half and roll out each half to a 33cm (13in) round.

3 Place one round on a greased baking tray. Spread the filling over the round. Dampen the edge and place the remaining dough on top. Pinch the edges together to seal. Leave it to prove in a warm place for 20–30 minutes, until the dough has puffed up.

4 Preheat the oven to 200°C/ 400°F/gas mark 6.

5 Brush the dough with extra oil and sprinkle with coarse salt. Bake for about 25 minutes, until it is golden brown. Serve hot, warm, or cold.

DOUGH

1 RECIPE QUICK-RISE PIZZA DOUGH (*SEE* PAGE 76),
    OR OTHER OF CHOICE, NOT PROVED

EXTRA VIRGIN OLIVE OIL

COARSE SEA SALT AND FRESHLY GROUND
    BLACK PEPPER

FILLING

1 LARGE RED ONION

1 GARLIC CLOVE

½ DRIED RED CHILLI

750G (1LB 10OZ) FRESH TENDER SPINACH

1 TBSP OLIVE OIL

115G (4OZ) STONED BLACK OLIVES, CHOPPED

3 TBSP FRESHLY GRATED PARMESAN

aubergine, red pepper, and black olive stuffed pizza

THIS RECIPE COMES FROM CAMPANIA AND THE FILLING IS A COMBINATION OF SICILIAN *CAPONATA* AND CAMPANIAN *PEPERONATA*. *PANZEROTTO* IS ANOTHER NAME FOR *CALZONE*, OR STUFFED PIZZA, SO THIS IS KNOWN AS *PANZEROTTO ALLA CAPONATA*. IT IS ASSOCIATED WITH THE FEAST OF ST GERARD, AS ARE A NUMBER OF BREAD- AND CHEESE-BASED DISHES.

DOUGH

1 RECIPE QUICK-RISE PIZZA DOUGH (*SEE* PAGE 76), OR OTHER OF CHOICE

1 SMALL EGG, BEATEN

2 TBSP DOUBLE CREAM

2 TBSP FRESHLY GRATED PARMESAN

FILLING

1 MEDIUM AUBERGINE, PEELED AND CUT INTO 2.5CM (1IN) CUBES

SEA SALT AND FRESHLY GROUND BLACK PEPPER

1 SMALL RED PEPPER

1 SMALL YELLOW PEPPER

3 TBSP OLIVE OIL

2 MEDIUM RED ONIONS, PEELED AND THINLY SLICED

3 TBSP WATER

1 TSP CASTER SUGAR

1 TBSP CAPERS, DRAINED AND RINSED

2 TBSP PINE NUTS

12 BLACK OLIVES, STONED AND CHOPPED

1 Preheat the oven to 200°C/ 400°F/gas mark 6.

2 Toss the aubergine with salt and place it in a colander to drain for 20 minutes.

3 Roast the peppers for 20 minutes. Cool and then skin them, cut them in half, remove the seeds, and cut the flesh into strips. Keep the oven on.

4 Heat half the oil over a low heat, add the onion and brown it for 8 minutes, stirring constantly. Add the water, sugar, some salt and pepper, the capers, pine nuts, olives, and pepper strips and toss until they are well blended.

5 Rinse the aubergine and dry it on kitchen paper. Heat the remaining oil over a medium heat

and sauté the cubes for 6–7 minutes, stirring constantly. Season with salt and mix with the onion mixture.

6 Put the knocked-back dough on a floured work surface and knead for 2–3 minutes. Roll into a 50cm (20in) circle that is 5mm (¼in) thick. Place the vegetables on one half of the circle, fold the dough over the filling, and press the edges together to seal them.

7 Mix the egg, cream, and cheese in a bowl, and brush the *calzone* with the mixture to cover all surfaces. Transfer it to a lightly greased baking sheet and bake it for 25 minutes.

8 Remove the bread from the oven, cut it into halves or quarters, and serve immediately.

sardinian pizza

THE PIZZA WAS BORN IN NAPLES, BUT IT HAS TRAVELLED ALL OVER MAINLAND ITALY AND THE ISLANDS, AND THIS VERSION IS PARTICULARLY POPULAR IN SARDINIA. THE SALTINESS OF THE ANCHOVIES GOES WONDERFULLY WITH THE NEW SEASON'S TOMATOES – BUT DON'T USE ANY CHEESE BECAUSE YOU DON'T NEED IT WITH FISH. THE PIZZA DOUGH IS SHORTER THAN OTHER DOUGHS BECAUSE IT IS ENRICHED WITH BUTTER AND EGG.

DOUGH

225G (8OZ) STRONG WHITE FLOUR

1 TSP FINE SEA SALT

65G (2¼OZ) UNSALTED BUTTER, SOFTENED
　　AND DICED

15G (½OZ) FRESH YEAST, CRUMBLED

4 TBSP WATER AT BODY TEMPERATURE

1 LARGE EGG, BEATEN

OLIVE OIL

TOPPING

5 TBSP OLIVE OIL

750G (1LB 10OZ) ONIONS, PEELED AND
　　FINELY SLICED

500G (18OZ) RIPE TOMATOES, SKINNED
　　AND ROUGHLY CHOPPED

FINE SEA SALT AND FRESHLY GROUND
　　BLACK PEPPER

55G (2OZ) ANCHOVY FILLETS

A FEW BLACK OLIVES, HALVED AND STONED

A HANDFUL OF FRESH OREGANO LEAVES

1 To make the dough, mix the flour and salt in a large bowl. Rub in the butter until the texture is like bread crumbs and make a well in the centre. Dissolve the yeast in the water and add it to the well in the flour, with the egg. Mix to a firm but pliable dough, adding more water if needed.

2 When the dough has come away cleanly from the sides of the bowl, turn it out onto a lightly floured surface and knead it thoroughly for 10 minutes. Gather it into a ball, place in a clean oiled bowl, and cover with a damp tea towel. Leave to rise until it has doubled in size: about 1½ hours.

3 Meanwhile, make the topping. Heat the olive oil in a heavy pan and fry the onion gently, covered, stirring now and then, until it is soft: about 20 minutes. Add the tomatoes, salt, and pepper and

cook, uncovered, until the sauce is thick: about another 20 minutes. Leave to become cold.

4 When the dough has risen, knock it back and turn it out onto a floured surface. Divide into two and knead each piece lightly for 2–3 minutes. Pat then stretch the pieces to a thickness of 1cm (½in) and a diameter of about 25cm (10in). (Or put it in two well-oiled 20–23cm/8–9in pizza tins and press out with floured knuckles.) Cover with a damp tea towel and leave to prove for 10 minutes.

5 Preheat the oven to 200°C/ 400°F/gas mark 6.

6 Spread the cold topping evenly on the two pizzas. Criss-cross them with strips of anchovy and add the olives. Sprinkle with oregano and bake for 25 minutes, until it is golden brown and bubbling.

tomato, onion, and rocket focaccia

THIS FOCACCIA, WITH ITS THUMBPRINT TOP, HAS A MOIST, HERB-SCENTED MIDDLE. MAKE SURE YOU PROPERLY PINCH THE EDGES OF THE DOUGH TO SEAL IN THE FILLING SO THAT IT CANNOT SPILL OUT.

1 Preheat the oven to 200°C/400°F/gas mark 6. Put the whole tomatoes in a roasting tin (without oil) and roast for 20 minutes.

2 Meanwhile, peel and roughly chop the onions. Heat 1 tbsp of oil in a frying pan, add the onion, and fry for about 5 minutes, until it is softened. Season with salt and pepper. Chop the mozzarella.

3 Knock the dough back, knead it on a lightly floured surface for 2–3 minutes, then divide it into two pieces. Roll out each piece of dough to a thin, 33cm (13in) round. Place one round on an oiled baking sheet.

4 Spread the onions over the round. Add the tomatoes and then the cheese. Sprinkle with rocket and oregano. Dampen the edge and cover with the second round of dough. Pinch the edges together and, using your fingertips, dimple the surface. Cover with a damp tea towel and leave to prove in a warm place for 20 minutes, until it has puffed up a bit.

5 Drizzle the remaining oil over the dough and sprinkle with coarse salt. Transfer it to a hot baking sheet, pizza stone, or bricks and bake, at the same temperature as above, for 25 minutes, until it is golden. Serve warm.

DOUGH

1 RECIPE SIMPLE FOCACCIA DOUGH (*SEE* PAGE 36), OR OF CHOICE

FILLING

450G (1LB) CHERRY TOMATOES

2 RED ONIONS

3 TBSP OLIVE OIL

COARSE SEA SALT AND FRESHLY GROUND BLACK PEPPER

175G (6OZ) MOZZARELLA CHEESE

1½ HANDFULS ROCKET LEAVES

3 TSP FINELY CHOPPED FRESH OREGANO

RISING: 1 hour   **PROVING:** 10 minutes   **BAKING:** 10–15 minutes   **DRIED YEAST:** 1 tsp

MAKES: 1 pizza roll (to serve 6–10 as canapés)

pizza roll

THIS ROLLED AND SLICED PIZZA IS A DISTINCTLY SOUTHERN ITALIAN DISH. IT CAN BE FILLED WITH YOUR CHOICE OF INGREDIENTS, BUT TYPICALLY IT WOULD HAVE MEAT, GREENS, AND CHEESE INSIDE. IT IS VERY VERSATILE AND CAN BE SERVED AS NIBBLES OR CANAPÉS, AS WELL AS FOR A MEAL.

DOUGH

1 RECIPE QUICK-RISE PIZZA DOUGH (*SEE* PAGE 76), OR OTHER OF CHOICE, JUST KNEADED, DIVIDED INTO TWO CHUNKS

OLIVE OIL

FILLING

3 TBSP OLIVE OIL

½ ONION, PEELED AND FINELY CHOPPED

200G (7OZ) SPINACH LEAVES

125G (4½OZ) RICOTTA CHEESE

SEA SALT AND FRESHLY GROUND BLACK PEPPER

175ML (6FL OZ) TOMATO PASSATA

250G (9OZ) BUFFALO MOZZARELLA, SLICED 1CM (½IN) THICK

1 Put each ball of dough in a separate, lightly oiled bowl. Turn each to coat it with oil. Cover with clingfilm or a damp cloth and leave to rise in a warm place for 1 hour, until it has doubled in size.

2 Meanwhile, for the filling, heat the olive oil in a frying pan over a medium heat. Add the onion and sauté it until it has softened: about 3–4 minutes. Add the spinach leaves and cook until they are wilted: about another 3 minutes. Remove from the heat, stir in the ricotta, and season with salt and pepper. Set aside to cool a little.

3 Knock back the pieces of dough and knead on a lightly floured surface for 2–3 minutes. Flatten one piece into a rectangle about 30 x 45cm (12 x 18in). Repeat with the second piece of dough. Cover each with a damp tea towel and leave to prove for 10 minutes.

4 Preheat the oven to 200°C/ 400°F/gas mark 6 and, if you have one, place a pizza stone inside. Otherwise preheat a heavy baking sheet.

5 Pat and stretch each piece of dough to a thickness of 1cm (½in), keeping the rectangle shape. Place each piece on a flour-dusted pizza paddle. Spread a thin layer of the passata over each pizza, leaving a 1cm (½in) rim. Top with half of the spinach and ricotta mixture, then layer on half of the mozzarella.

6 Roll each piece up like a Swiss roll and slide it onto the pizza stone, seam-side down so that it doesn't unroll. Bake for 10–15 minutes or until the edges are golden brown.

7 Remove from the oven. Cut crosswise into 1cm- (½in-) thick slices and serve at once.

BIGA: 24 hours   **RISING:** 1½ hours   **PROVING:** 20 minutes   **BAKING:** 20 minutes   **DRIED YEAST:** ½ tsp (biga) and 1 tsp (dough)

MAKES: 1 loaf (to serve about 6)

sage and hazelnut focaccia

SOME OF ITALY'S BEST HAZELNUTS COME FROM PIEDMONT AND THEY TASTE WONDERFUL WITH WILD MOUNTAIN SAGE.
I FIRST ENCOUNTERED THIS FOCACCIA IN LIGURIA, A REGION FAMOUS FOR ITS HERBS. THERE, A LITTLE BAKERY MADE
HUGE SHEETS OF IT AND I DISCOVERED THAT THE BAKERS HAD PUT WINE IN THE DOUGH. THIS MAKES THE YEAST
LIGHTER, ALMOST LIKE AN EXTRA FERMENTATION.

1 Put the flour and salt into a large bowl and make a well in the centre. Dissolve the fresh yeast in 1 tbsp of the water. Add the yeast liquid, chopped sage leaves, olive oil, and *biga* to the well in the flour and mix. Add the wine and enough of the remaining water to mix to a soft, sticky dough.

2 Turn the dough out onto a floured surface and knead until it is smooth, silky, and elastic: about 10 minutes. Place the dough in a clean oiled bowl, cover with a damp tea towel, and leave to rise until it has doubled in size: about 1½ hours.

3 Knock the dough back, put it on a lightly floured surface, and chafe, then rest for 10 minutes. Roll it out to approximately 1cm

(½in) in thickness. Place it on an oiled baking sheet, cover, and leave to prove until it has doubled in size: about 20 minutes.

4 Meanwhile, preheat the oven to 200°C/400°F/gas mark 6.

5 Press on the top of the dough with your fingers to form dimples. Sprinkle with olive oil, sea salt, fresh sage leaves, and toasted hazelnuts. Bake for 20 minutes or until it is golden brown and it sounds hollow when tapped on the base with the fingertips. Remove from the oven and sprinkle with extra olive oil.

DOUGH

375G (13OZ) STRONG WHITE FLOUR

1½ TSP FINE SEA SALT

10G (¼ OZ) FRESH YEAST, CRUMBLED

85ML (3FL OZ) WATER AT BODY TEMPERATURE

20 FRESH SAGE LEAVES, CHOPPED

3 TBSP OLIVE OIL

½ RECIPE *BIGA* (*SEE* PAGE 12)

85ML (3FL OZ) WHITE WINE

TOPPING

OLIVE OIL

COARSE SEA SALT

ABOUT 10 FRESH SAGE LEAVES, TORN

150G (5½OZ) SKINNED HAZELNUTS, TOASTED

olive bread with onion filling

THE ONIONS OF TROPEA IN CALABRIA ARE FAMOUS THROUGHOUT ITALY. THEY HAVE A SHORT SEASON, SO IF YOU COME ACROSS THEM BE SURE TO BUY THEM ON THE SPOT BECAUSE THEY ARE DELICIOUS, AS ARE THE GAETA OLIVES USED HERE. IF YOU CAN RESIST EATING THIS BREAD IMMEDIATELY, IT ALSO TASTES VERY GOOD TOASTED THE NEXT DAY.

DOUGH

500G (18OZ) STRONG WHITE FLOUR

5G (⅛OZ) FINE SEA SALT

15G (½OZ) FRESH YEAST, CRUMBLED

275ML (9½FL OZ) WATER AT BODY TEMPERATURE

2 TBSP OLIVE OIL

75G (2½OZ) GAETA OLIVES, OR THE BEST YOU CAN
    GET, STONED, SLICED, AND DRAINED

FILLING

2 TBSP OLIVE OIL

3 RED ONIONS, PEELED AND CHOPPED

2 BAY LEAVES

1 SPRIG FRESH ROSEMARY, LEAVES PICKED FROM
    THE STALKS

2 TBSP RED WINE VINEGAR

55G (2OZ) SOFT BROWN SUGAR

TO FINISH

A FEW FRESH ROSEMARY LEAVES

OLIVE OIL

COARSE SEA SALT

1 Sieve the flour and salt onto a work surface and make a well in the centre. Dissolve the yeast in the warm water. Add it and the olive oil to the well and slowly incorporate the flour to form a dough.

2 Knead the dough on a lightly floured surface for 10–15 minutes, until it is smooth and elastic. Add the olives and knead or chafe until they are evenly distributed. Put the dough in a lightly oiled bowl, cover with a damp tea towel, and leave for 40 minutes to double in size.

3 Meanwhile, heat the oil for the filling and brown the onions, bay leaves, and rosemary over a low to medium heat, stirring to prevent sticking. Add the vinegar and stir well. Add the sugar and cook over a low heat for 30 minutes. The mixture should be thick, shiny, and rich red. Allow to cool. (It can be kept in the fridge for two days.)

4 Knock back the dough, then knead it on a lightly floured surface for 2–3 minutes. Divide it in two and shape into balls. Cover and leave to relax for 10 minutes.

5 Roll each ball out into a long, flat oval shape. Place half the onion mixture and a few extra rosemary leaves slightly off-centre on each. Fold each piece over and pinch the edges together. Lightly brush the tops with olive oil and sprinkle with rock salt and rosemary leaves.

6 Place the dough on a lightly greased baking tray, cover with a damp tea towel, and leave to prove for 40 minutes.

7 Preheat the oven to 200°C/ 400°F/gas mark 6.

8 Bake the breads for 25 minutes, until they are golden. Brush with olive oil and cool on a wire rack.

spinach, olive, and onion flatbread

THIS IS A *TESTO* BREAD. *TESTO* MEANS "TILE", SO THIS IS A "BREAD OF THE TILE". IT HAILS FROM UMBRIA, WHERE FISHERMEN ON LAKE TRASIMENO, FISHING FOR PIKE, USED TO COOK IT AS A SNACK ON HOT STONES HEATED ON THE FIRE. THERE ARE NUMEROUS TRADITIONAL FILLINGS, BUT THE BREAD DOUGH IS ALWAYS THE SAME.

1 Sift the flour and salt into a large bowl, mix, and make a well in the middle. Mix the yeast with 1 tbsp of water. Pour the yeast liquid, olive oil, and some of the water into the well in the flour. Mix together, gradually adding the rest of the water, to form a soft dough.

2 Turn the dough onto a lightly floured work surface and knead vigorously for 10 minutes, until it is smooth. Put it in a clean bowl, cover with a damp tea towel, and leave in a warm place for 45 minutes to double in size.

3 Knock the dough back, and knead for 1–2 minutes. Return it to the bowl, cover, and leave to rise for about another 40 minutes.

4 Meanwhile, for the filling, heat the olive oil in a frying pan. Add the onion, garlic, and chilli and cook for about 5 minutes. Add

the spinach and cook for another 5 minutes, until it has wilted. Take it off the heat, add the olives, and season with salt and pepper. Allow to cool. Mix in the mozzarella.

5 Knock the dough back again and knead for 2–3 minutes on a lightly floured surface. Divide it in half and roll out each piece to a 33cm (13 inch) round. Place one on a lightly oiled baking sheet and spoon the filling on top, leaving a margin around the edge. Dampen the edge, cover with the second round, and pinch the edges together. Cover with a damp tea towel and leave to prove for 30 minutes.

6 Preheat the oven to 200°C/ 400°F/gas mark 6.

7 Drizzle the *testo* with olive oil and sprinkle with salt. Bake for 25 minutes, then cool on a wire rack. Serve hot, warm, or cold in wedges.

DOUGH

500G (18OZ) STRONG WHITE FLOUR

2 TSP FINE SEA SALT

15G (½OZ) FRESH YEAST

250ML (9FL OZ) WATER AT BODY TEMPERATURE

3 TBSP OLIVE OIL

FILLING

2 TBSP OLIVE OIL

1 LARGE RED ONION, PEELED AND SLICED

1 GARLIC CLOVE, PEELED AND CRUSHED

½ DRIED LONG, THIN RED CHILLI
    (*PEPERONCINO*), CRUSHED

750G (1LB 10OZ) SPINACH, TRIMMED, WASHED
    AND FINELY CHOPPED

115G (4OZ) STONED GREEN OLIVES, CHOPPED

SEA SALT AND FRESHLY GROUND BLACK PEPPER

85G (3OZ) MOZZARELLA CHEESE, DICED

FINISH

OLIVE OIL

COARSE SEA SALT

ham and black pepper flatbread

THIS 12TH-CENTURY FLATBREAD WITH A FILLED CRUST COMES FROM MY VILLAGE, MINORI IN CAMPANIA, AND THERE ARE MANY RECIPES FOR IT. I THINK YOU WILL ALTER THIS RECIPE AS YOU GROW USED TO IT – IT'S EASILY ADAPTABLE. YOU CAN SERVE IT HOT OR COLD, CUT INTO WEDGES – IT'S GREAT FOR PICNICS.

DOUGH

350G (12OZ) STRONG WHITE FLOUR

2 TSP FINE SEA SALT

15G (½OZ) FRESH YEAST, CRUMBLED

250ML (9FL OZ) WATER AT BODY TEMPERATURE

2 TBSP MELTED UNSALTED BUTTER

3 TSP FRESHLY GROUND BLACK PEPPER

FILLING

4 LARGE EGGS, HARD-BOILED, PEELED AND DICED

200G (7OZ) PARMA HAM, DICED

6 TBSP MELTED UNSALTED BUTTER

1 Mix the flour and salt into a heap on the work surface and make a well in the centre. Dissolve the yeast in 2 tbsp of the water. Add the yeast liquid, butter, 2 tsp of the pepper, and the remaining water to the well. Beat with a fork, incorporating a little flour at a time until a solid ball has formed.

2 Knead on a lightly floured surface for 10–15 minutes or until the dough is smooth and elastic. Lightly butter a bowl and put the dough in it, cover with a damp tea towel, and leave to rise for 1 hour.

3 Meanwhile, put the diced egg, ham, and 2 tbsp of the melted butter in a bowl and set aside.

4 Preheat the oven to 200°C/ 400°F/gas mark 6. Butter a 25cm (10in) round baking tin with 5cm (2in) high sides (or you can make the loaf free-form, as opposite).

5 Knock the dough back, then knead for 2–3 minutes. Shape into a large circle. Baste with half the remaining butter and fold the dough in half. Reshape. Create the original circle and dust the surface with the remaining black pepper. Knead for 5 minutes, or until the ingredients are well incorporated, and shape into a 30cm (12in) circle. Arrange in the tin and press the excess dough against the sides, coming up and over them. Cover and leave to prove for 10 minutes.

6 Spoon the egg, ham, and butter mixture around the edges only of the dough casing, then work the overlapping edges over the filling to enclose it and make a rolled crust. The middle will be plain dough.

7 Brush with half the remaining butter and bake for 20 minutes, until golden, basting the top two or three times with more butter.

flatbread with buffalo mozzarella and rosemary

THIS ONE IS A REAL HIT WITH THE LITTLE ONES — PARTICULARLY ANTONIA, MY DAUGHTER. IT'S PERFECT AS AN APPETIZER BEFORE A MEAL, AND IS ALSO A GOOD CHOICE FOR CHILDREN'S PARTIES.

DOUGH

300G (10½OZ) ITALIAN "00" PLAIN FLOUR

1 TSP SALT

10G (¼OZ) FRESH YEAST, CRUMBLED

500ML (18FL OZ) WATER AT BODY TEMPERATURE

3 TBSP OLIVE OIL

TOPPING

2 X 100G BALLS BUFFALO MOZZARELLA, WELL DRAINED AND GRATED.

SEA SALT AND FRESHLY GROUND BLACK PEPPER

APPROX. 2 TBSP EXTRA VIRGIN OLIVE OIL, OR TO TASTE

3 SPRIGS FRESH ROSEMARY, FINELY CHOPPED, OR TO TASTE

1 Put the flour and salt into a large bowl and make a well in the centre. Dissolve the yeast in some of the water and add it to the well in the flour, along with the olive oil and the rest of the water. Mix well to a soft dough.

2 Knead the dough on a lightly floured work surface for 10 minutes. The mixture will be soft and pillowy. Place it in a clean, lightly oiled bowl, cover with a damp tea towel, and leave to rise for 1 hour.

3 Knock back the dough and knead for 2–3 minutes on a lightly floured surface. Cover and leave it for a further 10 minutes to rest.

4 Pull out eight balls of the dough, with your fingertips, into very thin circles about 30cm (12in) in diameter.

5 Preheat the grill. Cook the dough circles one by one under the hot grill for about 2 minutes on each side, until they bubble and brown. Remove them to a chopping board and sprinkle them with mozzarella while they are still hot. Lightly sprinkle with salt and pepper, extra virgin olive oil, and rosemary.

6 Cut into wedges and devour.

flatbread with grapes

THIS SWEET PIZZA IS TYPICAL OF TUSCANY, WHERE I FIRST ENJOYED IT. SOMETIMES IT HAS FENNEL SEEDS SPRINKLED OVER THE TOP AND, SERVED WITH A DOLLOP OF MASCARPONE ON THE SIDE, IS THE ITALIAN EQUIVALENT OF AN ENGLISH CREAM TEA. IT IS ALSO GOOD AS A SNACK, SERVED WITH A GLASS OF WINE OR EVEN WITH CHEESE.

1 Put the raisins in a bowl, pour over the wine, and leave to soak for at least 2 hours. (You can do this the night before making the bread.)

2 Meanwhile, in a large bowl, mix the flour, salt, and 55g (2oz) of the sugar and make a well in the centre. Cream the yeast with the warmed milk then add this liquid to the well in the flour. Mix to form a soft dough.

3 Turn the dough onto a lightly floured work surface and knead for 10 minutes, until it is smooth. Put it in a bowl, cover with a damp tea towel, and leave in a warm place for 1 hour, until it has doubled in size.

4 Knock the dough back and knead it again for 1–2 minutes on a lightly floured surface. Drain the raisins.

5 Divide the dough into two even pieces. Roll out each piece to a 20cm (8in) round. Place one round on a floured baking sheet. Cover the round with half of the grapes and half of the drained raisins. Dampen the edge, cover with the second round, and seal. Top with the remaining grapes and raisins. Cover and leave to prove in a warm place for about 20 minutes, until it has doubled in size.

6 Preheat the oven to 180°C/ 350°F/gas mark 4.

7 Sprinkle the dough with the remaining sugar, then bake it for about 45 minutes, until it is golden. Cool it slightly before serving warm.

DOUGH

350G (12OZ) STRONG WHITE FLOUR

A PINCH OF FINE SEA SALT

85G (3OZ) GOLDEN CASTER SUGAR

10G (¼OZ) FRESH YEAST, CRUMBLED

150ML (5FL OZ) MILK, GENTLY WARMED

FILLING AND TOPPING

200G (7OZ) RAISINS

150ML (5FL OZ) VIN SANTO OR A SWEET DESSERT WINE

500G (18OZ) BLACK GRAPES, SEEDED

savoury breads

MOST OF THE BREADS IN THIS BOOK ARE SAVOURY, BUT I THINK OF THE BREADS IN THIS CHAPTER MORE AS "BUSY" BREADS: THEY ARE ESSENTIALLY PLAIN DOUGHS THAT HAVE BEEN ENRICHED WITH A MULTITUDE OF ADDITIONS. IN FACT, BECAUSE THESE BREADS ARE SO ENRICHED ALREADY, MOST WOULD NOT BENEFIT FROM A STARTER SUCH AS A *BIGA*, SO THERE IS NO ADVICE HERE ON MAKING SLOWER VERSIONS OF THE BREADS. BUT WHAT I COULD SAY IS THAT THESE RECIPES SHOULD ACT AS A BASIS UPON WHICH YOU CAN CREATE IDEAS OF YOUR OWN. MY FRIEND BRIDGET'S ROASTED GARLIC AND COURGETTE BREAD IS A CASE IN POINT: SHE CAME UP WITH THE IDEA BECAUSE HER SON SO LIKED THE BASIC VEGETABLE DISH. YOU COULD DO THE SAME WITH OTHER VEGETABLES OR COMBINATIONS.

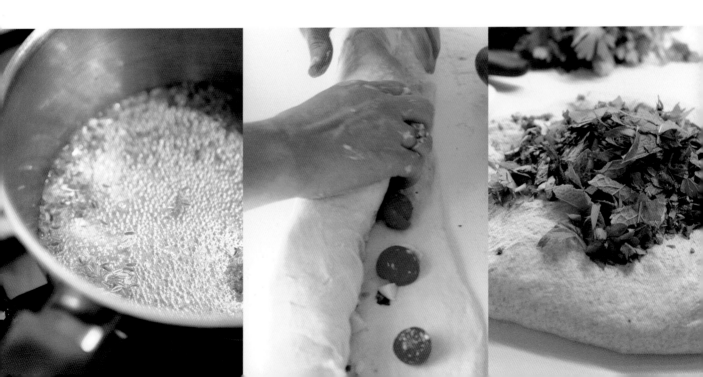

MANY OF THESE RECIPES USE INGREDIENTS THAT ARE UNUSUAL FOR BREADS – INCLUDING BAY LEAVES,
GORGONZOLA, CURRY PASTE, MANGO CHUTNEY, AND A NUMBER OF SPICES, TO NAME BUT A FEW! – BUT THERE
ARE ALSO PLAINER BREADS THAT ARE MADE WITH A LESS USUAL GRAIN, SUCH AS SPELT OR POLENTA.

THESE BREADS ARE SIMPLE TO MAKE YET MANY OF THEM ARE VERY VISUALLY IMPRESSIVE. THEY ARE ALSO
SATISFYING BREADS SUITABLE FOR MANY USES AND OCCASIONS. THEY ARE WONDERFUL IN A CHILD'S PACKED
LUNCH, TAKEN ON A PICNIC, OR EATEN AS PARTNERS FOR CHEESE OR SOUP – AND I THINK THEY WOULD BE
PERFECT FOR LADIES WHO LUNCH, TO ACCOMPANY A GOOD SALAD...

anise and bay crown loaf

THIS RECIPE EVOLVED OUT OF SHEER NECESSITY AND MY LOVE OF ANISE SEEDS AND BAY LEAVES. I THOUGHT THE TWO
WOULD MARRY WELL — AND INDEED THEY DO. THE BREAD LOOKS WONDERFUL, AS WELL. IT IS GOOD SERVED WITH
VERY SAVOURY FOODS BUT IS EQUALLY DELICIOUS TOASTED FOR BREAKFAST. I'VE SERVED IT WITH CHEESE AT THE
END OF A MEAL AND THAT'S BEEN POPULAR, TOO.

1 Put the anise seeds and water in a small pan and boil for 5 minutes. Pour the mixture into a large bowl and stir in the honey and milk. Let it cool down to body temperature.

2 Sprinkle the yeast over the liquid and stir until it has completely dissolved. Add the flour 115g (4oz) at a time and add the salt. Use only enough flour to make a soft dough.

3 Turn the dough onto a lightly floured board and knead for 10 minutes, adding flour as necessary to stop it from sticking. The dough should be smooth and tender. Put it in a large bowl and drizzle the olive oil over it. Cover with a damp tea towel and leave to rise for an hour or until it has doubled in size.

4 When the dough is ready, knock it back, turn it out onto a lightly floured board, and knead

for 2 minutes. Flour it lightly, cover it again with the tea towel, and let it rest for 5 minutes.

5 Roll the dough into a 28cm-(11in-) long rope. Twist the rope several times and arrange it in a ring on the baking sheet. Pinch the ends together and tuck them under. Make 10 diagonal slashes on the surface and tuck a bay leaf into each slash. Cover the dough and let it prove for 25–30 minutes.

6 Preheat the oven to 200°C/400°F/gas mark 6. Oil a large baking sheet.

7 Make the egg wash by beating the yolk and water in a small bowl. Brush it over the dough.

8 Bake for 30–35 minutes, until it is golden and the base sounds hollow when tapped.

DOUGH

1 TSP ANISE SEEDS

250ML (9FL OZ) SPRING WATER

1 TBSP CLEAR HONEY

250ML (9FL OZ) FULL-FAT MILK, WARMED

10G (¼OZ) FRESH YEAST, CRUMBLED

500–550G (18–20 OZ) STRONG WHITE FLOUR

3 TSP FINE SEA SALT

2 TBSP OLIVE OIL

10 BAY LEAVES

EGG WASH

1 LARGE EGG YOLK

1 TSP WATER

roasted garlic and courgette bread

MY FRIEND BRIDGET'S SON OLIVER SO LOVED HIS MOTHER'S COURGETTES STIR-FRIED WITH GARLIC THAT SHE TRIED INCORPORATING THEM INTO A BREAD. THE RECIPE WORKED MAGNIFICENTLY AND OLIVER WAS DOUBLY PLEASED!

1 GARLIC BULB

500G (18OZ) STRONG WHITE FLOUR

1½ TSP FINE SEA SALT

15G (½OZ) FRESH YEAST, CRUMBLED

225ML (8FL OZ) WATER AT BODY TEMPERATURE

2 TBSP OLIVE OIL

4 MEDIUM COURGETTES

COARSE SEA SALT

EXTRA VIRGIN OLIVE OIL

1 Preheat the oven to 200°C/400°F/gas mark 6. Put the garlic in a small baking tray and roast for 15–20 minutes. Leave to cool and switch the oven off.

2 Put the flour and salt in a large bowl and make a well in the centre. Cream the yeast with 1 tbsp of the water, then add to the well in the flour with the olive oil and remaining water. Mix until the dough comes away from the sides of the bowl.

3 Tip the dough onto a lightly floured surface and knead for 5 minutes, until it is smooth and elastic. Leave it to rise in a lightly oiled bowl, covered with a damp tea towel, for 1 hour or until it has doubled in size.

4 Meanwhile, grate the courgettes onto a clean tea towel and thoroughly squeeze out all the excess water. Put them in a bowl.

5 Squeeze the roasted garlic out of each clove and mix with the courgettes. Knock the dough back and knead and chafe the courgettes and garlic purée into the dough until they are evenly incorporated.

6 Mould the dough into a torpedo shape and turn the ends under. Drizzle lightly with olive oil and sprinkle with coarse sea salt. Cover and leave to prove for a further hour, until it has doubled in size.

7 Preheat the oven to 200°C/400°F/gas mark 6.

8 Bake the loaf for 20–30 minutes, until it is golden and the base of the bread sounds hollow when tapped. Drizzle it with extra virgin olive oil while it is still warm.

rye, dill, and crème fraîche loaf

THIS BREAD IS LOVELY SLICED THINLY, BUTTERED, AND SERVED WITH SMOKED SALMON. IT IS EQUALLY DELICIOUS TOASTED OR SERVED AS *CROSTINI*. GO ON – TREAT YOURSELF!

1 Put the flours into a large bowl. Stir in the dill, lemon zest, salt, and sugar and make a well in the centre. Dissolve the yeast in 1 tbsp of the water then pour this into the well in the flour. Mix in along with the crème fraîche and enough of the remaining water to make a smooth dough.

2 Tip the dough onto a lightly floured surface and knead for 5 minutes, until it is smooth and elastic. Place it in a lightly oiled bowl, cover with a damp tea towel, and leave to rise for 1 hour, until it has doubled in size.

3 Knock the dough back, then tip it onto a lightly floured surface and knead once more for 5 minutes, before shaping it into a round loaf. Place the loaf on a lightly greased baking sheet and make three cuts across the top with a sharp knife. Cover and leave it to prove for 30 minutes.

4 Preheat the oven to 200°C/ 400°F/gas mark 6.

5 Bake the bread for 25–30 minutes, until it has browned and the base sounds hollow when tapped with your fingertips. Cool on a wire rack.

175G (6OZ) RYE FLOUR

175G (6OZ) WHOLEMEAL FLOUR

115G (4OZ) STRONG WHITE FLOUR

2 TBSP FINELY CHOPPED FRESH DILL

FINELY GRATED ZEST OF 1 UNWAXED LEMON

2 TSP FINE SEA SALT

25G (1OZ) DARK SOFT BROWN SUGAR

10G (¼OZ) FRESH YEAST, CRUMBLED

250ML (9FL OZ) WATER AT BODY TEMPERATURE

150ML (5FL OZ) CRÈME FRAÎCHE

RISING: 1 hour **PROVING:** 30 minutes **BAKING:** 20–25 minutes **DRIED YEAST:** 2½ tsp **MAKES:** 1 loaf

tomato and mozzarella crown loaf

THIS IS A COLOURFUL AND DELICIOUS VARIATION ON THE *COURONNE* LOAF DESCRIBED ON PAGE 37. IT IS GREAT FOR

PICNICS OR PARTIES (PERHAPS AS ROLLS; *SEE* VARIATION ON PAGE 110) AND IS SURE TO BE LOVED BY THE CHILDREN.

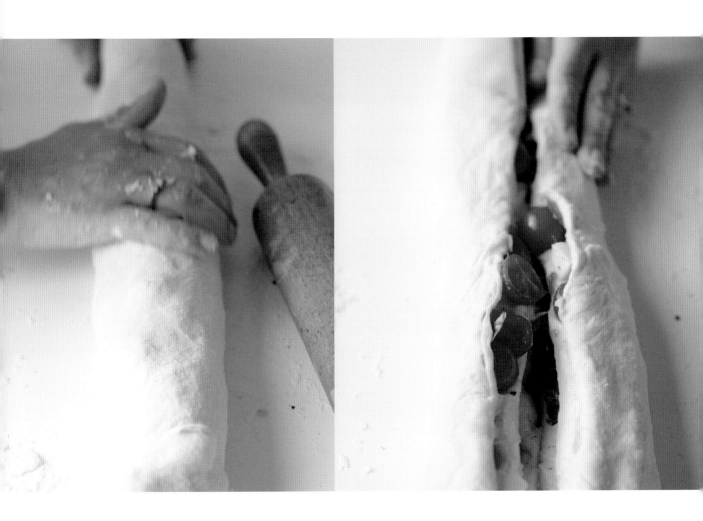

1 RECIPE *COURONNE* DOUGH (*SEE* PAGE 37),
   RISEN FOR 1 HOUR

115G (4OZ) CHERRY TOMATOES, HALVED

1 X 115G (4OZ) BALL MOZZARELLA,
   DRAINED AND CHOPPED

A HANDFUL OF FRESH BASIL, TORN

1 Knock the dough back, then
knead it on a lightly floured
surface for 2–3 minutes. Roll it
into a rectangle approximately
25 x 33cm (10 x 13in). Cover
the dough with the tomatoes,
mozzarella, and basil. Roll it
up from the long side until
it resembles a Swiss roll. Roll it
slightly, then cut lengthways along
the dough, not quite to the end.
You will have two long pieces
joined at one end; plait them
together. Twist into a circle shape,
pressing the ends to join.

2 Place the dough on a lightly
greased baking sheet. Grease a
small bowl and place it in the
centre of the bread to keep
the shape. Leave it to rise,
covered with a damp tea towel,
for 30 minutes, until it has
doubled in size.

3 Preheat the oven to 220°C/
425°F/gas mark 7.

4 Remove the bowl. Bake the
bread for 20–25 minutes, until it is
well risen and golden and the base
sounds hollow when tapped with
your fingertips. Cool it a little on
a wire rack, then serve and eat
warm (but it's good cold, too).

variation

You could make this mixture
into rolls. Divide the dough
into 12 balls and bake them for
10–25 minutes. Or the loaf could
be made free-form on a greased
baking sheet or in an oiled 900g
(2lb) loaf tin.

braided pepper biscuits

I FIRST ENJOYED THESE HARD BISCUITS IN PUGLIA MANY, MANY YEARS AGO, WITH FAMILY FRIENDS MARIO AND LUISA CARPENTIEI. THE BISCUITS CAN BE EATEN BEFORE LUNCH WITH DRINKS OR JUST AS A *MERENDA* (SNACK) AND ARE DELICIOUS WITH CHUNKS OF PARMESAN CHEESE. THERE ARE SO MANY VARIATIONS ON THIS RECIPE – SOMETIMES THE BISCUITS ARE PLAIN; SOMETIMES THEY ARE FLAVOURED WITH FENNEL SEEDS, FOR INSTANCE. ALL ARE GREAT, AND THEY MAKE GOOD GIFTS, TOO. THEY CAN BE MADE UP TO A WEEK IN ADVANCE AND KEPT IN A SEALED CONTAINER.

350G (12OZ) STRONG WHITE FLOUR

2 TSP FINE SEA SALT

3 TSP FRESHLY GROUND BLACK PEPPER

10G (¼OZ) FRESH YEAST

50ML (2FL OZ) WATER AT BODY TEMPERATURE

100G (3½OZ) UNSALTED BUTTER, MELTED

2 TBSP COARSE POLENTA

1 Heap the flour on a work surface, mix in the salt and pepper, and make a well in the centre. Dissolve the yeast in 2 tbsp of the water and pour it into the well in the flour with the melted butter. Stir with a fork, incorporating a little flour each time and adding more of the remaining water as needed to form a firm dough. Some flour may remain.

2 Knead the dough on a lightly floured surface for 15 minutes or until it is smooth and soft.

3 Pinch off a walnut-sized piece of dough and roll it into a 20cm (8in) rope. Holding one end in each hand, twist your right hand forward and your left hand backward, as if forming a rolled cord. Seal the two ends together to create a circle and place the dough

on a floured board. Continue until all the dough is used up, spacing the twisted circles well apart. Cover the dough with a damp tea towel and leave it to rise for 1¼ hours, until it has doubled in size.

4 Preheat the oven to 190°C/ 375°F/gas mark 5. Sprinkle the baking trays with polenta.

5 Transfer the dough circles to the baking trays, spaced well apart, and bake for 40 minutes. Remove from the oven and cool completely on wire racks before serving.

chestnut and hazelnut spiral bread

THIS BREAD GOES WELL WITH A RICH GAME STEW OR BOEUF BOURGUIGNON. IT IS ALSO GOOD SERVED

AS A FESTIVE BREAD – WITH GOOSE, PERHAPS, AT CHRISTMAS – OR AS ROLLS (*SEE* VARIATION BELOW).

1 Put the flour and salt into a large bowl and make a well in the centre. Cream the yeast with 1 tbsp of the water and add it to the flour with the remaining water. Mix until the dough comes away from the sides of the bowl.

2 Tip the dough out onto a lightly floured surface and knead for 5 minutes, until it is smooth. Place the dough in a lightly oiled bowl, cover with a damp tea towel, and leave to rise for 1 hour, until it has doubled in size.

3 Knock the dough back, then tip it out onto a lightly floured surface and knead for 5 minutes, until it is smooth and elastic. Place the chestnut purée and hazelnuts on top of the dough and knead and chafe them in until they are evenly distributed. Shape the dough into

a sausage about 30cm (12in) long, tapering at each end. Roll it into a flat coil, place on a greased baking sheet, and leave to prove, covered with a damp tea towel, for 1 hour, until it has doubled in size.

4 Preheat the oven to 200°C/ 400°F/gas mark 6.

5 Dust the loaf with extra flour and bake it for 20–25 minutes, until it is golden and the base of the bread sounds hollow when tapped with your fingertips. Cool it on a wire rack.

variation

This dough can be made into rolls. Divide it into 12 pieces, roll them into balls, or make knots, and bake them for 10–12 minutes.

500G (18OZ) STRONG WHITE FLOUR

1 TSP FINE SEA SALT

15G (½OZ) FRESH YEAST, CRUMBLED

250ML (9FL OZ) WATER AT BODY TEMPERATURE

1 X 435G CAN SWEET CHESTNUT PURÉE

115G (4OZ) SHELLED HAZELNUTS, TOASTED
    AND ROUGHLY CHOPPED

RISING: 1 hour **PROVING:** 1 hour **BAKING:** 25–30 minutes **DRIED YEAST:** 2½ tsp **MAKES:** 1 loaf

herb spelt bread

SPELT IS AN ANCIENT ROMAN GRAIN, A FORM OF WHEAT, THAT IS ENJOYING A RESURGENCE IN ITALY AND ELSEWHERE. IT IS VALUED AS A GRAIN THAT IS GOOD FOR THOSE WHO ARE GLUTEN OR WHEAT INTOLERANT, BUT IT IS WORTHY OF MUCH MORE WIDESPREAD ATTENTION THAN THAT BECAUSE IT IS DELICIOUS, WITH A NUTTY FLAVOUR AND GOOD TEXTURE.

1 Put the flour and salt in a large bowl and make a well in the centre. Dissolve the yeast in 1 tbsp of the water, then add it to the well in the flour with the olive oil and enough of the remaining water to make a firm dough.

2 Knead it for 5 minutes on a lightly floured surface, until it is soft to the touch. Leave it to rise in a clean oiled bowl, covered with a damp tea towel, for 1 hour.

3 Knock the dough back and knead it for 2–3 minutes on a lightly floured surface. Chop the herbs finely, place them on top of the dough, then knead or chafe them into the dough (shown opposite) until they are well incorporated. Shape the dough into a loaf and place it in an oiled 450g (1lb) loaf tin. Leave to prove, covered with a damp tea towel, for 1 hour, until it has doubled in size.

4 Preheat the oven to 220°C/ 425°F/gas mark 7.

5 Bake the loaf for 25–30 minutes, until it is golden and the base sounds hollow when tapped with your fingertips. Cool it on a wire rack.

variation

You can vary the herbs used: the herbs here are rather summery, but you could use sage, rosemary, and parsley, for instance.

500G (18OZ) SPELT FLOUR

1 TBSP FINE SEA SALT

20G (¾OZ) FRESH YEAST, CRUMBLED

400ML (14FL OZ) WATER AT BODY TEMPERATURE

2 TBSP OLIVE OIL

1 SMALL BUNCH FRESH BASIL

1 SMALL BUNCH FRESH FLAT-LEAF PARSLEY

1 SMALL BUNCH FRESH MINT

curry bread

THE IDEA FOR THIS BREAD WAS GIVEN TO MY FRIEND BRIDGET BY A FRIEND OF HERS WHO LOVES CURRY BUT IS NOT A FAN OF *NAAN* BREADS. IF YOU PREFER *NAAN*, YOU CAN MAKE THE DOUGH INTO FLATBREADS (SEE VARIATION BELOW).

300ML (10FL OZ) MILK

15G (½OZ) UNSALTED BUTTER

25G (1OZ) FRESH YEAST, CRUMBLED

450G (1LB) STRONG WHITE FLOUR

1 TSP FINE SEA SALT

1 TSP CUMIN SEEDS

1 TBSP MEDIUM CURRY PASTE

1 TBSP FRESH CORIANDER LEAVES, CHOPPED

1 TBSP MANGO CHUTNEY

1 LARGE EGG, BEATEN

MILK AND CUMIN SEEDS, FOR GLAZING

1 Heat the milk and butter together, then allow the mix to cool until it is tepid. Dissolve the yeast in a little of it.

2 Sift the flour and salt into a large bowl. Stir in the cumin seeds and make a well in the centre. Stir in the yeast liquid, curry paste, coriander, chutney, and egg, then pour in the remaining warmed milk-and-butter mixture and mix to a smooth dough.

3 Tip the dough out onto a lightly floured work surface and knead it for 10 minutes, until it is smooth and elastic. Leave it to rise in a lightly oiled bowl, covered with a damp tea towel, until it has doubled in size: about 1 hour.

4 Knock the dough back, then knead it on a lightly floured surface for a further 5 minutes. Shape it into a torpedo. Slash it down the middle of the loaf with a sharp knife about three times,

then brush it with milk and sprinkle with cumin seeds. Cover and leave to prove for 30 minutes on a lightly greased baking sheet until it is well risen.

5 Preheat the oven to 200°C/400°F/gas mark 6.

6 Bake the loaf for 30 minutes, until it is golden and sounds hollow when tapped on the base with your fingertips. Leave it to cool a little on a wire rack, then eat while it is still warm.

variation

You could make naan-like flatbreads from this mixture to go with your curry. Divide the dough into 12, then roll out to thin discs about 13cm (5in) long. Bake them for 12–15 minutes.

bacon, egg, and cheese bread

MY FRIEND BRIDGET FIRST MADE THIS BREAD WITH A COLLEAGUE AT LEITHS SCHOOL OF FOOD AND WINE WHEN SHE WAS TRAINING. IT HAS SINCE BECOME A FIRM FAVOURITE IN HER HOUSEHOLD AND IS REALLY A MEAL IN ITSELF.

1 Sift the flour and salt into a large bowl and make a well in the centre. Dissolve the yeast in a little of the water, then stir this yeasty liquid into the flour with enough of the remaining water to make a soft dough.

2 Knead the dough for 10–15 minutes on a lightly floured surface, until it is smooth and elastic. Place it in a lightly oiled bowl, cover with a damp tea towel, and leave to rise for 1 hour.

3 Knock the dough back, then tip it onto a lightly floured surface and knead for 2–3 minutes. Roll it to a rectangle roughly 25 x 33cm (10 x 13in). Cover the dough with the remaining ingredients, season with salt and pepper, and roll it into a sausage shape from the long

side. Place the seam underneath, and then tuck in each end. Place the loaf on a lightly greased baking sheet, cover with the damp tea towel, and leave to prove for 30 minutes, until it has doubled in size.

4 Preheat the oven to 200°C/ 400°F/gas mark 6.

5 Bake the loaf for 25–30 minutes, then leave it to cool on a wire rack.

variation

This mixture can be made into rolls. Divide the dough into 12 equal pieces and wrap them around the filling. Bake them for 12 minutes.

500G (18OZ) STRONG WHITE FLOUR

1½ TSP FINE SEA SALT

25G (1OZ) FRESH YEAST, CRUMBLED

500ML (18FL OZ) WATER AT BODY TEMPERATURE

115G (4OZ) BACON, RINDED, GRILLED, AND CHOPPED

4 LARGE HARD-BOILED EGGS, SHELLED, AND CHOPPED

115G (4OZ) GRUYÈRE CHEESE, FRESHLY GRATED

SEA SALT AND FRESHLY GROUND BLACK PEPPER

ricotta bread

THIS BREAD IS GOOD WITH CHEESE. IN THIS VERSION OF THE RECIPE, IT IS FLAVOURED WITH FENNEL SEEDS, BUT YOU COULD USE CRISPY BITS OF PANCETTA, WALNUTS, RAISINS, OR FIGS INSTEAD.

DOUGH

15G (½OZ) FRESH YEAST, CRUMBLED

225ML (8FL OZ) WATER AT BODY TEMPERATURE

1 X 125G TUB RICOTTA, AT ROOM TEMPERATURE

2 TSP FINE SEA SALT

A PINCH OF FENNEL SEEDS

500G (18OZ) STRONG WHITE FLOUR

2–3 TBSP OLIVE OIL

EGG WASH

1 LARGE EGG YOLK

1 TSP WATER

1 To make the dough, dissolve the yeast in some of the water in a large bowl. Stir in the ricotta, salt, and fennel seeds. Add the flour little by little, using only enough to make a soft dough.

2 Turn the dough out onto a lightly floured work surface. Knead it for 10 minutes, incorporating more flour if necessary to keep the dough from sticking. The dough should be smooth and tender. Transfer it to a large bowl and drizzle and rub olive oil over it. Cover the bowl with a damp tea towel and leave it for 1 hour, until the dough has doubled in size.

3 When the dough is ready, knock it back, turn it out onto a lightly floured work surface, and knead for 2 minutes. Flour the dough lightly and wrap and rest for 5 minutes.

4 Preheat the oven to 200°C/ 400°F/gas mark 6. Oil a large baking sheet.

5 Flatten the dough with a rolling pin and shape it into a 33 x 20cm (13 x 8in) oval. Transfer the dough to the baking sheet. Cut an 18cm (7in) long slit lengthwise through the centre of the dough, completely through the dough to the baking sheet. Spread the split open slightly. Cover the dough with a damp tea towel and let it prove for 15 minutes.

6 Make the egg wash by beating the egg yolk and water in a small bowl. Brush the egg wash over the surface of the dough. Bake the loaf on the centre shelf of the oven for 25–30 minutes or until it is rich brown and cooked through. Tap the bottom of the bread with your fingertips – it will sound hollow if it is done. Cool it on a wire rack.

RISING: 1½ hours   **PROVING:** 30 minutes   **BAKING:** 25 minutes   **DRIED YEAST:** 1 tsp

MAKES: 1 loaf that cuts into about 12 slices

onion and mozzarella bread

THROUGHOUT ITALY, *PALIOS* — HISTORICAL CONTESTS BETWEEN RIVAL TOWNS — ARE FOUGHT BETWEEN RIDERS ON HORSES, RIDERS ON DONKEYS, AND EVEN RIDERLESS PIGS. BUT IN GESSATE, IN LOMBARDY, THE *PALIO DEL PANE* IS FOUGHT BETWEEN PEOPLE ARMED WITH BUCKETS OF WATER, SALT, FLOUR, AND YEAST — ALL THE INGREDIENTS NECESSARY TO BAKE BREAD. THE SUBSEQUENT PEACE IS EXPRESSED IN VARIOUS TYPES OF BREAD THAT ARE MADE AND OFFERED TO THE SPECTATORS — AMONG THEM, THIS WONDERFULLY LIGHT RING TOPPED WITH SAUTÉED ONIONS AND FRESH MOZZARELLA.

1 RECIPE QUICK-RISE PIZZA DOUGH (*SEE* PAGE 76), OR OTHER OF CHOICE

3 TBSP OLIVE OIL

100G (3½OZ) UNSALTED BUTTER

3 LARGE RED ONIONS, PEELED AND THINLY SLICED

FINE SEA SALT

½ TSP CASTER SUGAR

1 TBSP COARSE POLENTA

250G (9OZ) FRESH MOZZARELLA, CUT INTO STRIPS

1 Put the risen pizza dough on a floured work surface and make a large hole in the centre without breaking through the underside. Pour in the oil. Knead it for 5 minutes or until the oil is completely incorporated. Transfer it to an oiled bowl, cover with a damp tea towel, and leave to rise for a further half-hour.

2 Heat the butter in a frying pan over a low heat and sauté the onion for 8 minutes, stirring frequently. Season with a pinch of salt and the sugar.

3 Sprinkle a 25 x 30cm (10 x 12in) baking sheet with the polenta. Knock the dough back and knead it on a lightly floured surface for 2–3 minutes. Form it into a long, thick sausage shape. Roll into a ring and press the ends

together to seal them. Transfer it to the baking sheet and coat with polenta. Cover with the tea towel and leave to prove for 30 minutes.

4 Preheat the oven to 200°C/ 400°F/gas mark 6.

5 Make a large hollow on the surface of the dough circle and fill it with the sautéed onions. Top with the strips of mozzarella and bake it for 25 minutes.

6 Remove the bread from the oven, cool it on a wire rack, and serve it hot or cold, cut into thick slices.

variation

You could make rolls with this mixture. Enclose the filling in small balls of dough and bake them for 10–12 minutes.

potato and gorgonzola focaccia

ON A BOOK-SIGNING AND PUBLICITY TOUR OF THE USA, I MET DIANE, THE MOTHER OF A FRIEND IN CHICAGO (MOTHER AND DAUGHTER ARE FINE COOKS). I WAS DOING A COOKERY DEMONSTRATION AND, AT THE END OF THE EVENING, DIANE PRESSED THIS RECIPE INTO MY HAND AND URGED ME TO TRY IT. I DID AND IT'S WONDERFUL. I THANK HER VERY MUCH.

1 In a covered saucepan, boil the potatoes for 10–15 minutes or until they are tender. Drain and mash them, then cool slightly.

2 In a large bowl, mix two thirds of the flour with the salt. Dissolve the yeast in 2 tbsp of the water and add it to a well in the centre of the flour with the olive oil. Mix for a few minutes, then stir in the potatoes and as much of the remaining flour as you can.

3 On a lightly floured surface, knead in enough of the remaining flour to make a stiff dough that is smooth and elastic. This will take about 8–10 minutes. Shape the dough into a ball and place it in an oiled bowl, turning it once to grease the surface. Cover it with a damp tea towel and leave it to rise in a warm place until it has doubled in size: roughly 1 hour.

4 Knock back the dough, cover, and let it rest for 10 minutes.

5 Grease a 38 x 25 x 2.5cm (15 x 10 x 1in) baking pan. Press the dough into the pan; if it is sticky, sprinkle the surface with about 1 tbsp of extra flour. Using your fingertips, make small indentations in the dough. Cover and leave it to prove until it has nearly doubled in size: 30 minutes.

6 Meanwhile, preheat the oven to 190°C/375°F/gas mark 5.

7 For the topping, mix the tomatoes, oregano, basil, garlic, and pepper and spoon evenly over the dough. Place the artichoke hearts over the tomato-sauce mixture. Cover with the Gorgonzola and shredded mozzarella.

8 Bake for 35 minutes. Serve hot.

DOUGH

2 MEDIUM POTATOES, PEELED AND CHOPPED

500–550G (18–20OZ) STRONG WHITE FLOUR

2 TSP FINE SEA SALT

15G (½OZ) FRESH YEAST, CRUMBLED

250ML (9FL OZ) WATER AT BODY TEMPERATURE

2 TBSP OLIVE OIL

TOPPING

1 X 400G CAN CHOPPED ITALIAN
    TOMATOES, DRAINED

1 TBSP CHOPPED FRESH OREGANO

2 TBSP TORN FRESH BASIL

1 GARLIC CLOVE, PEELED AND FINELY CHOPPED

½ TSP FRESHLY GROUND BLACK PEPPER

375G (13OZ) QUARTERED ARTICHOKE HEARTS
    MARINATED IN OLIVE OIL

250G (9OZ) GORGONZOLA CHEESE, CRUMBLED

150G (5½OZ) MOZZARELLA, SHREDDED

sweet breads

I HAVE A SWEET TOOTH, SO THIS IS AN IMPORTANT CHAPTER FOR ME! MANY OF THE BREADS HERE ARE NOT ACTUALLY "SWEET", IN TERMS OF HAVING A HIGH SUGAR CONTENT, BUT BECAUSE THEY ARE PACKED FULL OF DRIED FRUIT THEY ARE QUITE SWEET IN FLAVOUR. A NUMBER OF THESE BREADS ARE ACTUALLY FOR EATING IN A SAVOURY CONTEXT — WITH CHEESE OR DIPS (THE WALNUT BREAD, FOR INSTANCE).

THERE ARE IDEAS HERE FROM VARIOUS COUNTRIES, INCLUDING ITALY, THE USA, FRANCE, ENGLAND, AND SCOTLAND. I HAVE TO SAY THAT THE PRUNE AND CHOCOLATE BREAD ON PAGE 134 IS A REAL ALL-TIME FAVOURITE OF MINE — OOZING, GOOEY, DELICIOUS — AND I LIKE TO THINK OF IT AS THE PERFECT PICK-ME-UP FOOD WITH A LITTLE LESS GUILT, BECAUSE

PRUNES ARE SO GOOD FOR YOU. THE OTHERS ARE LESS EXOTIC BUT THEY ARE ALL GREAT BREADS, GOOD
FOR EVERYDAY MEALS, FOR SPECIAL OCCASIONS, AND ESPECIALLY FOR BREAKFAST AND TEATIME.

HOME-MADE BREADS, PARTICULARLY THE MORE UNUSUAL ONES, MAKE VERY GOOD GIFTS. THERE IS
NOTHING QUITE LIKE A PRESENT THAT SOMEONE HAS SPENT TIME AND EFFORT ON. MY NEIGHBOUR ANN RECENTLY
GAVE ME SOME DELICIOUS BREAD, AND I THOUGHT IT SUCH A NICE, NEIGHBOURLY THING TO DO. AND ONE OF
MY STUDENTS GAVE ME A SEMOLINA LOAF HE HAD BAKED FROM ONE OF MY BOOKS. I WAS VERY TOUCHED;
GIVING AND SHARING FOOD IS VERY SPECIAL.

treacle and date bread

THIS IS ONE OF MY FRIEND BRIDGET'S FAVOURITE BREADS AND WAS POPULAR WITH HER FRIENDS AND NEIGHBOURS WHEN SHE TESTED IT. MOST OF THEM AGREED THAT IT WAS LOVELY SERVED WITH BLUE CHEESE. SLICED AND SPREAD GENEROUSLY WITH BUTTER, IT IS WONDERFUL SERVED WITH A CUP OF TEA AT THE END OF A BUSY DAY.

1 Sift the flours and salt into a large bowl. Some grains from the wholemeal flour will be caught in the sieve – tip them into the bowl. Rub in the butter, and make a well in the centre. Dissolve the yeast in 2 tbsp of the water, then pour it into the well in the flour, along with the treacle and enough of the remaining water to form a soft smooth dough.

2 Tip the dough out onto a lightly floured surface and knead it for 10–15 minutes, until it is smooth and elastic. Leave the dough to rise in a lightly oiled bowl, covered with a damp tea towel, for 1 hour, until it has doubled in size.

3 Knock the dough back, then knead it on a lightly floured surface for 2–3 minutes. Press the dates into the top of the dough

and knead or chafe them in until they are evenly distributed. Shape the dough into a round. Dust it heavily with extra white flour and score diagonal lines across the top to make diamond shapes. Leave it to prove for 30 minutes, covered with a damp tea towel, until it has doubled in size.

4 Preheat the oven to 220°C/ 425°F/gas mark 7.

5 Bake for 30–35 minutes, until it is golden and sounds hollow when tapped on the base with your fingertips. Cool it on a wire rack.

225G (8OZ) STRONG WHITE FLOUR

225G (8OZ) WHOLEMEAL FLOUR

1 TBSP FINE SEA SALT

55G (2OZ) UNSALTED BUTTER, SOFTENED
    AND DICED

25G (1OZ) FRESH YEAST, CRUMBLED

300ML (10FL OZ) WATER AT BODY TEMPERATURE

1 TBSP TREACLE

85G (3OZ) DRIED DATES, CHOPPED

beer and honey bread

THIS BREAD HAS A LOVELY FERMENTED SMELL AND FLAVOUR. IT TASTES PARTICULARLY GREAT WHEN SLICED THINLY AND SERVED WITH SOFT GOAT'S CHEESE, FRESH FIGS, AND A DRIZZLE OF HONEY.

55G (2OZ) UNSALTED BUTTER, SOFTENED

300ML (10FL OZ) BROWN ALE

1 TBSP RUNNY HONEY

225G (8OZ) WHOLEMEAL FLOUR

225G (8OZ) STRONG WHITE FLOUR

1 TSP FINE SEA SALT

25G (1OZ) FRESH YEAST, CRUMBLED

1 LARGE EGG, BEATEN

1 Preheat the oven to 200°C/ 400°F/gas mark 6. Lightly butter a 1kg (2¼lb) loaf tin.

2 In a saucepan, bring the ale, honey, and butter to boiling point and then leave the mixture to cool to body temperature.

3 Sift the flours and salt into a large mixing bowl. Some grains from the wholemeal flour will be caught in the sieve – tip them into the bowl and make a well in the centre. Dissolve the yeast in 1 tbsp of the beer liquid and pour it into the well in the flour, along with the beaten egg and the remainder of the beer liquid. Mix to a soft dough.

4 Knead the dough on a lightly floured surface for 10 minutes, until it is smooth and elastic. Put it into a lightly oiled bowl, cover with a damp tea towel, and leave to rise in a warm place for 1 hour, until it has doubled in size.

5 Knock the dough back, then tip it onto a lightly floured work surface and knead for 5 minutes. Shape it into a loaf and place in the prepared tin. Leave to prove, covered with a damp tea towel, for 30 minutes

6 Bake the loaf for 30–35 minutes, until it is golden and sounds hollow when tapped on the base with your fingertips. Cool it on a wire rack.

toffee and banana-filled doughnuts

THIS IS A STRAIGHTFORWARD RAINY-DAY RECIPE TO GIVE THE CHILDREN A FUN AND MEMORABLE TIME. THEY WILL ENJOY FILLING EACH DOUGHNUT WITH TOFFEE SAUCE AND WILL MAKE THEMSELVES SOME LOVELY, STICKY TREATS.

1 Sift the flour into a large bowl. Rub in the butter, then stir in 40g (1½oz) of the sugar and make a well in the centre. Dissolve the yeast in 2 tbsp of the water and pour it into the well with enough of the remaining water to make a smooth dough.

2 Tip the dough out onto a lightly floured work surface and knead it for 10–15 minutes, until it is smooth and elastic. Leave for 1 hour in a lightly oiled bowl, covered with a damp tea towel, until it has doubled in size.

3 Knock back the dough and knead it for 2–3 minutes on a lightly floured surface. Split it into 85g (3oz) pieces. Push 2 slices of banana into each piece and shape them into balls. Cover and leave to prove on a floured work surface for 30 minutes.

4 Heat the oil to 170°C/325°F in a large, heavy pan. Fry the dough balls in batches for 5–10 minutes, until they are golden. Drain well on kitchen paper.

5 Put the toffee sauce into a piping bag with a small nozzle. Pipe a little of toffee sauce into each doughnut, then dust them heavily with the remaining caster sugar. Cool them on a wire rack

250G (9OZ) STRONG WHITE FLOUR

25G (1OZ) UNSALTED BUTTER, SOFTENED
AND DICED

150G (5½OZ) CASTER SUGAR

25G (1OZ) FRESH YEAST, CRUMBLED

150ML (5FL OZ) WATER AT BODY TEMPERATURE

2 BANANAS, PEELED AND SLICED

SUNFLOWER OIL, FOR DEEP-FRYING

1 JAR TOFFEE SAUCE (DELICE IF YOU CAN GET IT)

lemon loaf

THIS BREAD IS LOVELY TOASTED WITH BUTTER AS A BREAKFAST BREAD, AND MY FRIEND BRIDGET'S DAUGHTER LOVES IT MADE INTO HONEY SANDWICHES FOR HER SCHOOL PACKED LUNCH.

400G (14OZ) STRONG WHITE FLOUR

100G (3½OZ) RYE FLOUR

1 TBSP FINE SEA SALT

70G (2½OZ) UNSALTED BUTTER, SOFTENED
    AND DICED

70G (2½OZ) CASTER SUGAR

25G (1OZ) FRESH YEAST, CRUMBLED

300ML (10FL OZ) WATER AT BODY TEMPERATURE

2 TBSP OLIVE OIL

FINELY GRATED ZEST OF 5 UNWAXED LEMONS

115G (4OZ) CANDIED LEMON PEEL, FINELY CHOPPED

1 Put the flours, salt, butter, and sugar into a large bowl. Rub the butter in until the mixture is like bread crumbs, then make a well in the centre. Cream the yeast with 1 tbsp of the water and add it to the flour with the olive oil and remaining water. Mix until the dough comes away from the sides of the bowl.

2 Tip the dough out onto a lightly floured surface and knead for 5 minutes, until it is smooth. Place it in a lightly oiled bowl, cover with a damp tea towel, and leave to rise for 1 hour, until it has doubled in size.

3 Knock the dough back, then knead it for 2–3 minutes on a lightly floured surface before kneading or chafing in the lemon zest and candied peel. Shape the dough into two round loaves and place them on a greased baking sheet. Make three cuts across each loaf, cover with a damp tea towel, and leave to prove for 1 hour, until they have doubled in size.

4 Preheat the oven to 200°C/ 400°F/gas mark 6.

5 Bake the loaves for 25–30 minutes, until they are golden brown and their bases sound hollow when tapped with your fingertips. Cool them on a wire rack.

lardy cake

THIS RECIPE WAS GIVEN TO MY FRIEND BRIDGET BY A NEIGHBOUR WHO ASSURES HER OF ITS AUTHENTICITY. BRIDGET WAS KEEN TO USE BUTTER INSTEAD OF LARD – BUT THEN, OF COURSE, IT WOULDN'T BE A LARDY CAKE. THIS VERSION OF THE RECIPE HAS FRUIT IN IT, ALTHOUGH SOME PEOPLE OMIT IT.

DOUGH

450G (1LB) STRONG WHITE FLOUR

1 TSP FINE SEA SALT

15G (½OZ) LARD, SOFTENED AND DICED

25G (1OZ) CASTER SUGAR

25G (1OZ) FRESH YEAST, CRUMBLED

300ML (10FL OZ) WATER AT BODY TEMPERATURE

FILLING

85G (3OZ) LARD, DICED

85G (3OZ) SOFT LIGHT BROWN SUGAR

115G (4OZ) RAISINS

115G (4OZ) SULTANAS

25G (1OZ) CANDIED LEMON PEEL, CHOPPED

1 TSP MIXED SPICE

GLAZE

2 TSP SUNFLOWER OIL

2 TBSP CASTER SUGAR

1 Sift the flour and salt into a large bowl and rub in the lard. Stir in the sugar and make a well in the centre. Dissolve the yeast in 2 tbsp of the water, pour it into the well, and add the remaining water gradually, mixing until you have a smooth dough.

2 Turn the dough out onto a lightly floured surface and knead it for 10 minutes, until it is smooth and elastic. Place it in a lightly oiled bowl, cover with a damp tea towel, and leave to rise for 1 hour.

3 Knock back the dough, then turn it out onto a lightly floured surface and knead for 2–3 minutes. Roll it into a rectangle. Using half the lard for the filling, cover the top two thirds of the dough with dots of lard. Sprinkle over half the sugar, half the dried fruits and peel, and half the mixed spice. Fold the

bottom third up and the top third down, pressing the edges together with a rolling pin. Turn the dough sideways. Roll lightly and cover with the remaining ingredients. Fold as before, then roll. Grease a 25 x 20cm (10 x 8in) Swiss-roll tin. Place the dough in the tin, cover it with a damp tea towel, and leave it to prove for 30–40 minutes.

4 Preheat the oven to 200°C/ 400°F/gas mark 6.

5 Brush the top with the oil and sprinkle over the sugar. Using a sharp knife, mark a diamond pattern over the top. Bake for 30–40 minutes. Leave the cake to cool in the tin, then cut it into squares to serve.

selkirk bannock

THIS RICH YEASTED CAKE-BREAD FROM THE SCOTTISH BORDERS IS STUFFED WITH DRIED FRUIT AND IS SAID TO HAVE
EVOLVED AS A WAY OF USING UP LEFTOVER BREAD DOUGH. SOME SAY IT IS THE SCOTTISH EQUIVALENT OF LARDY CAKE.

1 Mix together a little milk and 2 tsp of sugar for the glaze.

2 Put the flour and salt in a bowl and make a well in the centre. Dissolve the yeast and 1 tsp of sugar in a little of the milk and leave to froth. Melt the butter and lard with the rest of the milk and keep the liquid warm.

3 Mix the yeast liquid with the flour, then add the milk-and-butter mixture, and mix until it forms a soft dough. Knead for a few minutes on a lightly floured surface, then cover with a damp tea towel, and leave until it has doubled in size: about 1 hour.

4 Knock the dough back, then knead it on a lightly floured surface for 2–3 minutes before kneading or chafing in the rest of the sugar and the sultanas. Shape it into two rounds. Put onto an oiled baking sheet, cover again, and leave to prove, in a warm place, until it has doubled in size: about 45 minutes.

5 Preheat the oven to 220°C/ 425°F/gas mark 7.

6 Bake for 10 minutes, then reduce the heat to 190°C/375°F/ gas mark 5 for half an hour. After about 15 minutes, glaze the bannock with the reserved milk and the sugar dissolved in it.

400ML (14FL OZ) MILK AT BODY TEMPERATURE

175G (6OZ) CASTER SUGAR

1 KG (2¼LB) STRONG WHITE FLOUR

A PINCH OF FINE SEA SALT

25G (1OZ) FRESH YEAST, CRUMBLED

115G (4OZ) UNSALTED BUTTER

115G (4OZ) LARD

450G (1LB) SULTANAS

saffron and raisin breadsticks

SAFFRON IS PROBABLY THE MOST EXPENSIVE SPICE IN THE WORLD, WHICH MAKES THIS RECIPE RATHER A LUXURY, BECAUSE IT USES TWO WHOLE TEASPOONS OF IT. THE STICKS ARE GOOD AS SNACKS, OR WITH CHEESE, SOUP, OR DIPS.

1 Infuse the saffron with 2 tbsp of the warm milk and leave for 10 minutes.

2 Sift the flour, salt, sugar, and spices into a bowl, then rub in the butter until the mixture is like bread crumbs. Add the raisins and make a well in the centre. Dissolve the yeast in 2 tbsp of the milk and pour it into the well, along with the saffron liquid. Gradually add the remaining milk until you have a soft dough

3 Tip the dough onto a lightly floured work surface and knead for 5 minutes, until it is smooth and elastic. Place it in a lightly oiled bowl, cover with a damp tea towel, and leave to rise in a warm place until it has doubled in size: about 45 minutes.

4 Preheat the oven to 180°C/350°F/gas mark 4.

5 Knock the dough back, then tip it onto the floured surface and knead for 2–3 minutes. Divide the dough into 12 equal pieces and, after cleaning the surface to make it flour-free, pull each piece out to a 25cm (10in) stick. Place the sticks on a greased baking sheet.

6 Bake the breadsticks for 10-12 minutes. Cool on a wire rack.

variations

To make a single loaf, grease a 900g (1lb) loaf tin. After knocking the dough back, place it in the tin, cover it, and leave to prove for 30 minutes. Bake for about 40 minutes.

To make rolls, divide the knocked-back dough into 12 pieces and roll into balls. Prove for 30 minutes. Glaze with beaten egg and bake it for 25–30 minutes.

2 TSP SAFFRON STRANDS

300ML (10FL OZ) MILK AT BODY TEMPERATURE

450G (1 LB) STRONG WHITE FLOUR

¼ TSP FINE SEA SALT

115G (4OZ) CASTER SUGAR

¼ TSP MIXED SPICE

¼ TSP GROUND CINNAMON

175G (6OZ) UNSALTED BUTTER, SOFTENED AND DICED

225G (8OZ) RAISINS

25G (1OZ) FRESH YEAST, CRUMBLED

prune and chocolate bread

I ADORE PRUNES AND WISH THEY WERE TAKEN MORE SERIOUSLY. THEY ARE AN EXCELLENT SOURCE OF VITAMIN A WITH IRON AND FIBRE. THE COMBINATION OF PRUNES AND CHOCOLATE IS HEAVENLY. THIS IS A WONDERFUL BREAKFAST BREAD – IT IS RICH, SWEET, DARK, AND DELICIOUS, AND DOESN'T NEED ANYTHING ELSE WITH IT. TRY MAKING IT WITH HALF DARK CHOCOLATE AND HALF GOOD-QUALITY WHITE CHOCOLATE, TOO.

750G (1LB 10OZ) STRONG WHITE FLOUR OR
  HALF STRONG WHITE AND HALF STRONG
  WHOLEMEAL FLOUR

2 TSP FINE SEA SALT

20G (¾OZ) FRESH YEAST

450ML (16FL OZ) WATER AT BODY TEMPERATURE

350G (12OZ) STONED PRUNES

350G (12OZ) PLAIN CHOCOLATE

20G (¾OZ) UNSALTED BUTTER

1 LARGE EGG

1 Mix the flour and salt in a large bowl and make a well in the centre. Blend the fresh yeast with 2 tbsp of the water and add it to the well. Gradually add about three quarters of the rest of the water to the flour and mix well. The dough should be firm and leave the sides of the bowl clean. If it looks dry, add some of the remaining water.

2 Turn the dough out onto a lightly floured work surface and knead well for 10 minutes. You should have a smooth, elastic dough. Return it to a clean bowl, cover with a damp tea towel, and leave to rise in a warm place for 1 hour, until it has doubled in size.

3 Meanwhile preheat the oven to 220°C/425°F/gas mark 7. Grease two 900g (2lb) loaf tins.

4 Chop the prunes, chocolate, and butter. Beat the egg.

5 Knock the dough back, turn it onto a lightly floured work surface, and knead again for 2–3 minutes. Press the prunes, chocolate, butter, and beaten egg onto the top of the dough, then knead or chafe well for 10 minutes, so that they are evenly distributed. You may need a bit more flour if the dough is tacky.

6 Put half the dough in each tin. Cover with the damp tea towel and allow to prove for 10 minutes.

7 Bake the loaves for 35 minutes. The bread is ready if the base sounds hollow when tapped with your fingertips. Leave it to cool on a wire rack. Serve warm.

variation
You could make one large loaf and two smaller ones (in 450g/1lb tins), or you could free-form two oval loaves and bake on a greased baking sheet. The smaller loaves would take 20–25 minutes to bake.

alpine fruit bread

TOWNS IN THE ALTO ADIGE, THE PART OF ITALY THAT LIES IN THE ALPS, HOST OPEN-AIR MARKETS DURING THE CHRISTMAS SEASON, FEATURING A GREAT VARIETY OF ARTS AND CRAFTS. THIS TRADITIONAL CHRISTMAS FRUIT BREAD IS AVAILABLE TO BUY AT THESE MARKETS. IT'S WONDERFUL, PACKED FULL OF GOODIES, AND IF YOU HAVE ANY LEFT OVER YOU CAN USE IT TO MAKE A FANTASTIC BREAD-AND-BUTTER PUDDING (*SEE* PAGE 186).

100G (3½OZ) RAISINS

100G (3½OZ) CANDIED PEEL, DICED

75ML (2½FL OZ) GRAPPA

75ML (2½FL OZ) WATER

250G (9OZ) UNSALTED BUTTER

3 LARGE EGGS

150G (5½OZ) CASTER SUGAR

350G (12OZ) ITALIAN "00" PLAIN FLOUR

10G (¼OZ) FRESH YEAST, CRUMBLED

1 TBSP WATER AT BODY TEMPERATURE

100G (3½OZ) PINE NUTS

100G (3½OZ) GROUND ALMONDS

100G (3½OZ) PITTED DATES, SLICED

100G (3½OZ) WALNUT PIECES, CHOPPED

⅛ TSP GROUND CINNAMON

⅛ TSP GROUND CLOVES

3 TBSP WHOLE MILK

1 Soak the raisins and peel in the grappa for 1 hour.

2 Meanwhile, heat the water until it is boiling and add the butter. Stir until the butter melts. Keep warm.

3 Beat the eggs with the sugar in a bowl until they are smooth and creamy. Stir in the flour little by little. Dissolve the yeast in the water and add it to the flour mixture. Pour in the melted butter and stir until it is well blended. Drain the raisins and peel and add them to the dough with the pine nuts, almonds, dates, walnuts, cinnamon, cloves, and milk. Mix well, then put into a large, oiled bowl, cover with a damp tea towel, and leave to rise for 1 hour, until the dough has doubled in size.

4 Preheat the oven to 200°C/ 400°F/gas mark 6. Butter and flour a 30 x 40cm (12 x 16in) baking tray, shaking off the excess flour.

5 Shape the dough into four oval loaves about 2.5cm (1in) high. Place them on the prepared tray about 7.5cm (3in) apart, cover, and prove for 20 minutes.

6 Bake for 30 minutes or until a toothpick inserted in the centre comes out clean. Remove from the oven and cool to room temperature on a wire rack. Cut into thin slices and serve.

french spice bread

THIS IS A VERY CHRISTMASSY BREAD, WITH ALL THOSE WARM AND WARMING SPICES. IT IS DELICIOUS BY ITSELF OR TOASTED, OR, AS THE FRENCH WOULD SERVE IT, AS *PAIN PERDU* (DIPPED IN EGG AND MILK AND PAN-FRIED WITH A SPRINKLING OF VANILLA SUGAR AND A DRIZZLE OF HONEY). THE BREAD KEEPS WELL IF IT IS WELL WRAPPED.

1 Put the flour, salt, spices, and sugar into a large bowl and rub in the butter until the mixture resembles bread crumbs. Make a well in the centre. Cream the yeast with 1 tbsp of the warm milk and add to the flour with the eggs and the remaining milk until you have a dough that comes away from the sides of the bowl.

2 Tip the dough onto a lightly floured surface and knead for 5 minutes, until it is smooth. Place it in a lightly oiled bowl covered with a damp tea towel and leave it to rise for 45 minutes in a warm place, until it has doubled in size.

3 Knock back the dough and knead it for 2–3 minutes on a lightly floured surface. Press the

remaining ingredients onto the top of the dough, then knead or chafe until they are evenly distributed. Shape the dough into two round loaves. Place them on a greased baking sheet and leave to prove for 20–30 minutes, until they are risen.

4 Preheat the oven to 220°C/425°F/gas mark 7.

5 Using a sharp knife, slash each loaf three times across the top. Bake for 20 minutes, until they are golden. Cool on a wire rack.

500G (18OZ) STRONG PLAIN FLOUR

1 TBSP FINE SEA SALT

1 TSP GROUND CINNAMON

1 TSP GROUND CLOVES

115G (4OZ) CASTER SUGAR

85G (3OZ) BUTTER, SOFTENED AND DICED

25G (1OZ) FRESH YEAST, CRUMBLED

300ML (10FL OZ) MILK AT BODY TEMPERATURE

3 MEDIUM EGGS, BEATEN

FINELY GRATED ZEST OF 1 UNWAXED LEMON

FINELY GRATED ZEST OF 1 UNWAXED ORANGE

55G (2OZ) BLANCHED ALMONDS, CHOPPED

55G (2OZ) CANDIED LEMON PEEL, CHOPPED

55G (2OZ) RAISINS

walnut and raisin bread

THIS IS ANOTHER CLASSIC COMBINATION OF FLOURS, WITH WALNUT OIL INTENSIFYING THE FLAVOUR OF THE NUTS THEMSELVES. THIS BREAD IS GREAT ON A CHEESE BOARD — SOMETIMES A CRACKER JUST ISN'T ENOUGH AND YOU NEED A BREAD — AND I LOVE IT TOASTED FOR BREAKFAST. IT LASTS WELL, TOO.

1 Put the flours and salt into a large bowl and rub in the butter until the mixture resembles fine bread crumbs. Make a well in the centre. Cream the yeast with 2 tbsp of the water, then mix it into the well in the flour with the walnut oil and enough of the remaining water to make a soft dough.

2 Tip the dough onto a lightly floured surface and knead for 5 minutes, until it is smooth and elastic. Place it in a lightly oiled bowl, cover with a damp tea towel, and leave to rise for 1 hour, until it has doubled in size.

3 Knock back the dough, then turn it out onto a lightly floured surface and knead for 2–3 minutes. Press the walnuts and raisins into the top of the dough, then knead or chafe in until they are evenly distributed. Shape the dough into two torpedoes, then, using a sharp knife, make three diagonal cuts through the dough. Place the loaves on a greased baking sheet, cover, and leave to prove for 1 hour, until they have doubled in size.

4 Preheat the oven to 220°C/ 425°F/gas mark 7.

5 Bake the loaves for 25–30 minutes, until they are golden brown and their bases sound hollow when tapped with your fingertips. Cool them on a wire rack.

250G (9OZ) WHOLEMEAL FLOUR

250G (9OZ) STRONG WHITE FLOUR

1½ TSP FINE SEA SALT

40G (1½OZ) UNSALTED BUTTER, SOFTENED AND DICED

25G (1OZ) FRESH YEAST, CRUMBLED

300ML (10FL OZ) WATER AT BODY TEMPERATURE

4 TBSP WALNUT OIL

140G (5OZ) WALNUT PIECES, CHOPPED

115G (4OZ) RAISINS

RISING: 1 hour or longer **PROVING:** 40 minutes **BAKING:** 35 minutes **DRIED YEAST:** 2 tsp **MAKES:** 1 loaf

pine nut bread

THERE ARE MANY VARIATIONS OF THIS CLASSIC BREAKFAST BREAD FROM THE SOUTH OF ITALY: YOU CAN USE ALMONDS INSTEAD OF PINE NUTS, OR ALMONDS *AND* HAZELNUTS. IT'S YUMMY WHATEVER IT CONTAINS. WHEN I TAUGHT IN ITALY, I ALWAYS SERVED IT FOR BREAKFAST; I MADE THE DOUGH LAST THING AT NIGHT AND BAKED IT IN THE MORNING.

100G (3½OZ) SULTANAS

JUICE AND FINELY GRATED ZEST OF
   3 UNWAXED ORANGES

FINELY GRATED ZEST OF 1 UNWAXED LEMON

400G (14OZ) STRONG WHITE FLOUR

1¼ TSP FINE SEA SALT

150G (5½OZ) UNSALTED BUTTER, DICED

2 LARGE EGGS, BEATEN

15G (½OZ) FRESH YEAST, CRUMBLED

2½ TBSP WATER AT BODY TEMPERATURE

40G (1½OZ) SHELLED HAZELNUTS, TOASTED

75G (2¾OZ) PINE NUTS, TOASTED

ICING SUGAR, FOR DUSTING

1 Put the sultanas, orange and lemon zest, and orange juice in a bowl and leave to soak for 30 minutes.

2 Mix the flour and salt in a bowl. Rub in the diced butter with the tips of your fingers until the mixture looks like coarse crumbs. Make a well in the centre and add the beaten egg and soaked sultana mixture. Dissolve the yeast in the water and pour it into the well in the flour. Mix the yeast, eggs, and sultanas in the well, then gradually work in the flour to make a very soft, slightly sticky dough. Work in more tepid water if it's dry; you want a tacky dough.

3 Turn the dough out onto a floured work surface and knead for 5 minutes. Return the dough to a clean bowl, cover with a damp tea towel, and leave to rise until it has doubled in size: about 1 hour (or longer if you have time – even overnight in the fridge).

4 Knock the dough back, then turn it out onto a lightly floured work surface and knead for 2–3 minutes. Press the nuts onto the surface of the dough and gently knead or chafe them in. When they are evenly distributed, shape the dough into a ball, then pat it into a round about 20cm (8in) in diameter and 4cm (1½in) thick. Set the dough on a greased baking sheet, cover with a damp tea towel, and leave to prove for about 40 minutes.

5 Preheat the oven to 190°C/375°F/gas mark 5.

6 Bake the loaf for about 35 minutes, until it is golden brown and sounds hollow when the based is tapped with your fingertips. Transfer it to a wire rack and, when it is cool, dust it with icing sugar.

almond, cherry, and rosemary bread

THIS BREAD IS A MUST WITH A GOOD CHEESE SELECTION, AND IT'S ALSO VERY PLEASANT TOASTED FOR BREAKFAST OR AT TEATIME. DRIED CHERRIES CAN BE FOUND IN MOST SHOPS THESE DAYS, BUT IF YOU CAN'T GET THEM, USE SULTANAS OR RAISINS INSTEAD. THE RESULTING BREAD WILL STILL BE VERY GOOD.

1 Put the flours and salt into a large bowl. Rub in the butter until the mixture resembles bread crumbs, then make a well in the centre. Dissolve the yeast in 2 tbsp of the water and add it to the well. Mix, adding enough of the remaining water to make a smooth dough.

2 On a lightly floured work surface, knead the dough for 5 minutes, until it is smooth and elastic. Place it in a lightly oiled bowl, cover with a damp tea towel, and leave to rise for 1 hour, until it has doubled in size.

3 Knock the dough back and knead it on a lightly floured surface for 2–3 minutes. Push the almonds, cherries, and rosemary into the top of the dough, then knead or chafe until they are evenly distributed. Shape the dough into a round and place it on a greased baking sheet. Cover with a damp tea towel and leave to prove for 25 minutes.

4 Preheat the oven to 220°C/ 425°F/gas mark 7.

5 Bake the loaf for 25–30 minutes, until it has risen and is golden and the base sounds hollow when tapped with your fingertips. Leave it to cool on a wire rack.

variation

This dough could be made into rolls. Divide it into 12 pieces, shape them into balls, and bake for 10–12 minutes.

225G (8OZ) STRONG WHITE FLOUR

225G (8OZ) WHOLEMEAL FLOUR

1 TBSP FINE SEA SALT

55G (2OZ) UNSALTED BUTTER, SOFTENED AND DICED

25G (1OZ) FRESH YEAST, CRUMBLED

300ML (10FL OZ) WATER AT BODY TEMPERATURE

115G (4OZ) WHOLE BLANCHED ALMONDS, ROUGHLY CHOPPED

85G (3OZ) DRIED CHERRIES

LEAVES FROM 2 SPRIGS FRESH ROSEMARY, FINELY CHOPPED

RISING: 1 hour **PROVING:** 1 hour **BAKING:** 25–30 minutes **DRIED YEAST:** 3½ tsp **MAKES:** 1 loaf

pear and almond pain polka

THIS IS A QUICK VERSION OF A BREAD FROM THE LOIRE. IT LOOKS FANTASTIC, TOO. THE BREAD IS USUALLY SAVOURY AND IS TRADITIONALLY MADE WITH A *LEVAIN,* A FRENCH STARTER DOUGH. FEEL FREE TO USE OTHER FRUITS AND NUTS, AS DICTATED BY YOUR STORE CUPBOARD. WALNUTS, APRICOTS, AND FIGS WORK PARTICULARLY WELL.

1 Mix the flour, salt, sugar, and ground almonds in a large bowl and rub in the butter until the mixture is like bread crumbs. Make a well in the centre. Dissolve the yeast in a little of the milk and pour it into the well with the remaining milk. Mix to make a sticky dough.

2 Tip the dough out onto a lightly floured surface and knead it for 5 minutes, until it is smooth and elastic. Place the dough in a lightly oiled bowl, cover with a damp tea towel, and leave to rise for 1 hour, until it has doubled in size.

3 Knock back the dough, then knead it for 2–3 minutes on a lightly floured surface. Press the pears and half of the almonds on top of the bread, then knead or chafe until they are evenly distributed. Flatten the dough into a round shape, then make deep cuts on the top in a criss-cross pattern. Scatter over the remaining almonds. Place the dough on a greased baking sheet, cover with the damp tea towel, and leave to prove for 1 hour, until it has doubled in size.

4 Preheat the oven to 180°C/ 350°F/gas mark 4.

5 Bake the loaf for 25–30 minutes, until it has risen and is golden and the base of the bread sounds hollow when tapped with your fingertips. Cool on a wire rack. Using a spoon, drizzle with melted chocolate before serving.

450G (1LB) STRONG PLAIN FLOUR

1 TBSP FINE SEA SALT

55G (2OZ) CASTER SUGAR

85G (3OZ) GROUND ALMONDS

40G (1½OZ) UNSALTED BUTTER, SOFTENED
   AND DICED

25G (1OZ) FRESH YEAST, CRUMBLED

300ML (10FL OZ) WARM MILK

2 RIPE PEARS, PEELED, CORED, AND DICED

125G (4½OZ) FLAKED ALMONDS

75G (2½OZ) DARK CHOCOLATE, MELTED (OPTIONAL)

yeast-free breads

THE CHEMICAL LEAVENS UTILIZED IN THE RECIPES ARE QUICK, WITH NO TIME-CONSUMING RISING OR PROVING.

HOWEVER, EVEN WHEN TIME IS SHORT, YEAST REMAINS VERY IMPORTANT: BREADS RISEN BY YEAST ARE LIGHTER,

WITH, TO MY MIND, MORE INTERESTING TEXTURES AND FLAVOURS. BUT THE BREADS HERE ARE STILL PACKED FULL

OF FLAVOUR, AND I HAVE CHOSEN INTERESTING RECIPES. THERE ARE BREADS FROM IRELAND — THE HOME OF

SODA BREADS — ENGLAND, SCOTLAND, WALES, ITALY, AND ELSEWHERE.

THESE YEAST-FREE BREADS CAN BE MADE FROM INGREDIENTS THAT YOU PROBABLY ALREADY HAVE IN YOUR STORE CUPBOARD, AND MOST OF THEM ARE VIRTUALLY INSTANTANEOUS. A SODA BREAD, FOR INSTANCE, COULD BE MIXED JUST BEFORE YOU HAVE YOUR SHOWER IN THE MORNING, THEN BAKED IN TIME FOR BREAKFAST. AND I AM CONFIDENT THAT ONCE YOU HAVE TRIED THE OATCAKES (*SEE* PAGE 163) – THE CLASSIC SCOTTISH FLATBREADS – YOU WILL NEVER WANT TO BUY THEM READY-MADE AGAIN. WELCOME TO A WORLD OF QUICK AND EASY TREATS!

fried bread circles

THESE CRISP, YEAST-FREE DISCS CAN BE DRESSED WITH MANY TOPPINGS — I PARTICULARLY LIKE BUFFALO MOZZARELLA OR ANCHOVIES AND OLIVES. THEY ARE VERY QUICK AND EASY TO MAKE AND ARE GREAT FOR PARTIES.

1 Put the flour, salt, and bicarbonate of soda into a bowl, make a well in the centre, and mix in the milk until you have a firm dough.

2 Knead the dough lightly on a floured surface for 5 minutes. Cover the dough in the bowl with a damp tea towel and leave to rest for 45 minutes.

3 Break off small golf-ball-sized pieces of dough and roll them out to very thin discs of about 18cm (7in) in diameter.

4 Heat a large frying pan with the oil and fry the discs one at a time until they are crisp and golden: about 2 minutes each side. Drain them on kitchen paper.

5 Sprinkle the circles with coarse sea salt and top them with your chosen additions.

225G (8OZ) STRONG BREAD FLOUR

A PINCH OF FINE SEA SALT

A PINCH OF BICARBONATE OF SODA

125ML (4FL OZ) MILK

OLIVE OIL OR GROUNDNUT OIL,
    FOR SHALLOW-FRYING

COARSE SEA SALT

bara brith

THIS RECIPE FOR *BARA BRITH,* THE WELSH "SPECKLED BREAD", WAS GIVEN TO MY FRIEND BRIDGET BY HER GOOD FRIENDS RHYS AND JACKY. BECAUSE THE BREAD KEEPS WELL — AND FREEZES WELL — IT IS SENSIBLE TO MAKE TWO LOAVES AT THE SAME TIME.

175G (6OZ) DARK BROWN MUSCOVADO SUGAR

425ML (15FL OZ) MILK

150G (5½OZ) UNSALTED BUTTER, SOFTENED
    AND DICED

675G (1½LB) DRIED MIXED FRUIT

55G (2OZ) GLACÉ CHERRIES, CHOPPED

55G (2OZ) SHELLED WALNUTS, CHOPPED

325G (11OZ) SELF-RAISING FLOUR, SIFTED

1½ TSP BICARBONATE OF SODA

3 LARGE EGGS, BEATEN

1 Preheat the oven to 180°C/ 350°F/gas mark 4. Line two 900g (2lb) loaf tins with parchment paper.

2 Place the sugar, milk, butter, mixed fruit, cherries, and walnuts in a saucepan and simmer for 4 minutes. Allow to cool.

3 When the mixture is cool, stir in the sifted flour and bicarbonate of soda, then add the beaten eggs. Mix well.

4 Divide the mixture between the two lined tins. Place them side by side on the middle shelf of the oven and bake for about 1 hour. Pierce with a warmed skewer to test whether they are cooked through. If the skewer comes out clean, the cake is done. Leave it to cool in the tin.

marsala fruit-and-nut rolls

THIS IS KNOWN AS *ROCCIATA D'ASSISI* IN ITALY: *ROCCIATA* IS AN ALMOST LITERAL TRANSLATION OF *RUGELACH,* MEANING SMALL JEWISH PASTRIES ENCASING A VARIETY OF FRUITS AND NUTS. IN THIS DELICIOUS VERSION, HOWEVER, THE SLICES ARE LARGER AND THE PASTRY IS MADE FROM A THICKER, MORE ELASTIC DOUGH THAN USUAL.

PASTRY

300G (10½OZ) ITALIAN "00" PLAIN FLOUR

A PINCH OF SEA SALT

1 LARGE EGG, LIGHTLY BEATEN

1 TBSP OLIVE OIL

2–3 TBSP WATER AT BODY TEMPERATURE

FILLING

2 MEDIUM EATING APPLES, PEELED, CORED,
    AND THINLY SLICED

8 DRIED PRUNES, STONED AND CHOPPED

2 DRIED FIGS, STEMS REMOVED AND CHOPPED

55G (2OZ) PINE NUTS, CHOPPED

8 WALNUTS, SHELLED AND CHOPPED

8 HAZELNUTS, SHELLED AND CHOPPED

1 TSP FINELY GRATED UNWAXED LEMON ZEST

⅛ TSP GROUND CINNAMON

85G (3OZ) CASTER SUGAR

5 TBSP MARSALA WINE

FINISH

15G (½OZ) UNSALTED BUTTER TO GREASE TRAY

ASSORTED NUTS AND FRUIT TO GARNISH

1 To make the pastry, heap the flour and salt on a work surface and make a well in the centre. Add the egg, oil, and 1 tbsp of the water and mix with a fork, incorporating the flour a little at a time and adding more water as needed to form a soft, smooth dough (some flour may remain).

2 Knead the pastry for 10 minutes, then cover with a damp tea towel, and leave to rest for 1 hour.

3 Preheat the oven to180°C/ 350°F/gas mark 4. Butter a baking tray.

4 Put all the filling ingredients into a bowl, and mix until they are well blended.

5 Roll the pastry into a 40 x 50cm (16 x 20in) rectangle about 3mm (⅛in) thick. Distribute the fruit-and-nut mixture evenly over the surface, leaving a 4cm (1½in) border on all sides. Roll up from the short side and press the edges together to seal them. Arrange the roll in the buttered tray seam-side down.

6 Bake for 30 minutes. Remove from the oven and cool for 15 minutes. Cut into 2.5cm- (1in-) thick slices. Arrange on a plate and garnish with dried fruit and nuts.

rum plum bread

I SOMETIMES FANCY SOMETHING SWEET FOR LUNCH OR A SNACK, AND THIS PLUM BREAD USUALLY FITS THE
BILL. IT'S A FRUITY TEALOAF WITH LEMON AND SPICES AND, OF COURSE, RUM – AND IT'S VERY MOREISH!

1 Preheat the oven to 170°C/ 325°F/gas mark 3. Butter two 23 x 13 x 5cm (9 x 5 x 2in) loaf tins and line the bases with parchment paper.

2 Sift the flour, salt, and mixed spice into a large bowl, then mix in the lemon rind. Cut the butter into the flour and rub it in with your fingertips until the mixture resembles bread crumbs. Sift in the sugar and mix in well.

3 Break the eggs into a jug. Add the milk and rum and beat them to mix. Chop the prunes with a knife dipped into flour and mix with the raisins and sultanas.

4 Add the fruit and egg mixtures to the flour mixture and mix well.

5 Divide the mixture between the two tins and spread evenly. Bake for 1½ hours, until they are firm to the touch. Turn the loaves out of the tins and leave them to cool on a wire rack.

750G (1LB 10OZ) WHITE OR WHOLEMEAL
   SELF-RAISING FLOUR

1 TSP FINE SEA SALT

2 TSP GROUND MIXED SPICE

FINELY GRATED RIND OF 1 UNWAXED LEMON

225G (8OZ) UNSALTED BUTTER, DICED

350G (12OZ) MUSCOVADO SUGAR

4 LARGE EGGS

450ML (16FL OZ) MILK

4 TBSP DARK RUM

450G (1LB) STONED PRUNES
   (PREFERABLY UNSULPHURED)

225G (8OZ) RAISINS

450G (1LB) SULTANAS

quick individual gingerbreads

THIS IS MY FRIEND BRIDGET'S RECIPE AND I AM VERY PLEASED TO ADD IT TO MY REPERTOIRE. I USUALLY MAKE
SOMETHING SPECIAL ON SATURDAYS FOR TEA FOR MY HUSBAND, DAUGHTER, AND FATHER-IN-LAW – ONE WEEK I
MADE THESE AND THEY WERE A GREAT SUCCESS. THAT'S A HIGH RECOMMENDATION!

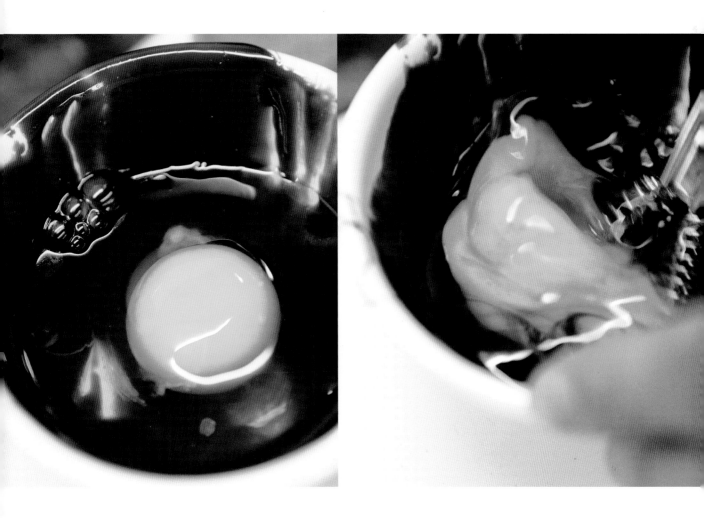

DRY INGREDIENTS

115G (4OZ) PLAIN FLOUR

1 TSP GROUND GINGER

½ TBSP GROUND CINNAMON

1 TSP BICARBONATE OF SODA

115G (4OZ) SOFT LIGHT BROWN SUGAR

55G (2OZ) STEM GINGER, FINELY CHOPPED

WET INGREDIENTS

115G (4OZ) UNSALTED BUTTER, MELTED

115G (4OZ) BLACK TREACLE

1 LARGE EGG, BEATEN

150ML (5FL OZ) MILK

1 Preheat the oven to 180°C/ 350°F/gas mark 4. Line a 12-hole muffin tin with muffin cases.

2 Place all the dry ingredients in a large bowl and mix thoroughly. Make a well in the centre.

3 Gently heat the butter and treacle together, until the butter melts. Stir in the egg and milk. Pour the wet ingredients into the well in the dry ones and mix well to incorporate all the ingredients.

4 Pour the mixture into the individual muffin cases. Bake for 15–20 minutes, until they have risen and are golden. Cool them on a wire rack.

quick corn and carrot muffins

THESE ARE GREAT TO MAKE WITH CHILDREN BECAUSE THEY REQUIRE VERY LITTLE EFFORT. YOU CAN ALSO VARY THE BASIC RECIPE BY ADDING CHOPPED SALAMI TO MAKE A MORE SUBSTANTIAL MUFFIN TO GO IN LUNCH BOXES.

1 Preheat the oven to 200°C/400°F/gas mark 6. Grease a 12-hole muffin tin and line it with parchment paper, or line 12 individual muffin cases.

2 Sift the flour, cornmeal, salt, and baking powder into a large bowl. Stir in the sugar, Cheddar, carrot, and sweetcorn. Make a well in the centre and pour in the butter, milk, and eggs. Season with salt and pepper. Mix until the ingredients are well combined.

3 Spoon the mixture into the muffin cases and bake for 20–30 minutes, until a skewer inserted into the centre comes out clean. Cool on a wire rack.

85G (3OZ) STRONG WHITE FLOUR

150G (5½OZ) FINE CORNMEAL

1 TSP FINE SEA SALT

1½ TSP BAKING POWDER

1 TBSP CASTER SUGAR

55G (2OZ) STRONG CHEDDAR, FRESHLY GRATED

55G (2OZ) GRATED CARROT

1 X 285G CAN SWEETCORN, DRAINED

55G (2OZ) UNSALTED BUTTER, MELTED

250ML (9FL OZ) MILK

3 LARGE EGGS, BEATEN

SEA SALT AND FRESHLY GROUND BLACK PEPPER

cheese scones

THIS WAS THE FIRST RECIPE MY FRIEND BRIDGET EVER COOKED, AT THE GRAND AGE OF SEVEN. HER GRANDPARENTS GAVE HER HER FIRST COOKERY BOOK, WHICH LATER INSPIRED HER TO GO ON WITH COOKING AS A CAREER. THESE SCONES ARE LOVELY EATEN WARM, SPLIT IN HALF AND SPREAD WITH LOTS OF BUTTER.

225G (8OZ) PLAIN FLOUR

A PINCH OF FINE SEA SALT

1 LEVEL TSP BICARBONATE OF SODA

2 LEVEL TSP CREAM OF TARTAR

55G (2OZ) UNSALTED BUTTER, SOFTENED
   AND DICED

85G (3OZ) STRONG CHEDDAR, FRESHLY GRATED

A PINCH OF CAYENNE PEPPER

150ML (5FL OZ) MILK

1 Preheat the oven to 220°C/ 425°F/gas mark 7. Lightly grease a baking sheet.

2 Sieve the flour, salt, bicarbonate of soda, and cream of tartar into a large bowl. Rub in the butter until the mixture resembles bread crumbs. Stir in the cheese and cayenne and make a well in the centre. Gradually add the milk, stirring with a table knife. Bring the mixture into a ball and turn it out onto a lightly floured surface.

3 Roll the dough to approximately 2.5cm (1in) in thickness and cut it into eight (or more) 5cm (2in) rounds.

4 Place the scones on the prepared baking sheet and brush their tops with a little extra milk. Bake for 8–10 minutes, until they are well risen and golden. Cool them a little on a wire rack before eating them warm.

variation

You can add about ½ tsp of dried mustard powder with the cayenne to make the scones a little spicier. My husband Richard loves this!

griddled flatbread

THIS IS A FLATBREAD FROM THE ITALIAN REGION OF EMILIA-ROMAGNA. IT IS OFTEN SOLD ON TAKE-AWAY STALLS IN THE STREETS, USUALLY WITH A CHOICE OF FILLINGS. I HAVE BEEN WAITING FOR A CHANCE TO PASS ON THIS RECIPE — PARTICULARLY NOW THAT I HAVE A VERSION THAT I REALLY LIKE AND THAT WORKS SO WELL.

1 In a large bowl, stir the flour, salt, and baking powder together. Using a pastry cutter or knife, cut in the butter until the mixture resembles bread crumbs. Make a well in the centre and add enough of the water to bring the dough together.

2 On a lightly floured work surface, knead the dough for a few seconds until it is smooth and not sticky. Divide it into eight equal pieces. Roll each into a 15cm (6in) round about 3mm (⅛in) thick.

3 Heat a heavy frying pan over a medium-high heat and brush it lightly with the olive oil. Cook the dough rounds for about 1 minute on each side or until they are lightly brown. Brush the frying pan with more oil as needed when cooking each round. Drain the rounds well on kitchen paper.

4 Sprinkle them with cheese, top with ham, and season with vinegar, oil, and black pepper. Fold in half and eat immediately.

200G (7OZ) STRONG WHITE FLOUR

½ TSP FINE SEA SALT

½ TSP BAKING POWDER

40G (1½OZ) UNSALTED BUTTER, SOFTENED AND DICED

125ML (4FL OZ) WATER AT BODY TEMPERATURE

3 TBSP OLIVE OIL

100G (3½OZ) PARMESAN SHAVINGS

8 THIN SLICES PARMA HAM

2 TSP GOOD-QUALITY BALSAMIC VINEGAR

2 TSP GOOD-QUALITY EXTRA VIRGIN OLIVE OIL

FRESHLY GROUND BLACK PEPPER

oatcakes

TRADITIONALLY OATCAKES ARE COOKED ON A *GIRDLE,* BUT THEY CAN BE BAKED IN THE OVEN. THE ROLLING AND CUTTING MUST BE DONE QUICKLY BECAUSE THE PASTE IS NOT EASILY WORKED ONCE IT COOLS DOWN. FOR THIS REASON, DON'T TRY TO MAKE LARGE AMOUNTS OF DOUGH — TO MAKE MORE CAKES, JUST REPEAT THE PROCESS UNTIL YOU HAVE ENOUGH.

1 Preheat a *girdle* (griddle) on the hob, or preheat the oven to 190°C/375°F/gas mark 5 with a baking sheet inside to heat up.

2 Mix the oatmeal with the salt and bicarbonate of soda. Pour in the melted fat and mix it in. Gradually add enough of the hot water to create a stiff paste, but go carefully – you don't want to use too much.

3 On a lightly floured board, roll out the mixture either into a circle to cut into quarters, or into a rectangle to cut into triangles.

4 Using a fish slice or spatula, place the oatcakes on the hot *girdle* or on the hot baking sheet. Bake until they are just browned at the edges: 8–10 minutes. Cool them on a wire rack and store in an airtight container.

115G (4 OZ) MEDIUM AND FINE OATMEAL, MIXED

A PINCH OF FINE SEA SALT

A PINCH OF BICARBONATE OF SODA

2 TSP MELTED LARD (OR UNSALTED BUTTER)

ABOUT 2–3 TBSP HOT WATER

irish oatmeal soda bread

THIS RECIPE HAS BEEN MADE FOR YEARS BY MY FRIEND BRIDGET'S MOTHER, WHO HAS PASSED IT ON TO BRIDGET
AND HER SISTERS — AND THEY ALL NOW MAKE IT FOR THEIR FAMILIES. IT'S PARTICULARY GREAT WITH CHEESE.

300G (10½OZ) WHOLEMEAL FLOUR

55G (2OZ) FINE OATMEAL

25G (1OZ) UNSALTED BUTTER, SOFTENED
    AND DICED

1 TSP BICARBONATE OF SODA

1 TSP FINE SEA SALT

1 TSP CASTER SUGAR

200ML (7FL OZ) BUTTERMILK OR NATURAL YOGURT

200ML (7FL OZ) MILK AT BODY TEMPERATURE

1 Preheat the oven to 200°C/ 400°F/gas mark 6. Grease a baking sheet.

2 Put the flour and oatmeal in a large bowl and rub in the butter until the texture is like bread crumbs. Stir through the bicarbonate of soda, salt, and sugar and make a well in the centre. Pour in the buttermilk or yogurt and milk and mix quickly to a dough. Free-form the dough into a round or oval and transfer it to the prepared baking sheet. Make a cross on the top using a floured wooden spoon handle, as shown opposite.

3 Bake for 25 minutes, covered lightly with foil. Remove the foil and bake for a further 25 minutes. Leave to cool in the tin.

variation
Grease a deep, 18cm (7in) square cake tin with extra butter and lightly dust with extra wholemeal flour. Ease the dough into the prepared tin and bake it as described above.

note
If you cannot find buttermilk in the shops, make a close equivalent at home. Mix 1 tbsp lemon juice (or cider vinegar) to 225ml (8fl oz) skimmed milk. Stir and let it stand for about 5 minutes, then use.

wholemeal soda bread

MY FRIEND BRIDGET'S MOTHER USED TO MAKE THIS REGULARLY BECAUSE SHE HAD EIGHT HUNGRY CHILDREN TO FEED. IT'S ONE OF THE SIMPLEST BREADS GOING AND IS GREAT FOR CHILDREN TO MAKE.

225G (8OZ) PLAIN FLOUR

225G (8OZ) WHOLEMEAL FLOUR

1 TSP FINE SEA SALT

2 TSP BICARBONATE OF SODA

2 TSP CREAM OF TARTAR

45G (1½OZ) UNSALTED BUTTER, SOFTENED
    AND DICED

1 TSP CASTER SUGAR

350–375ML (12–13FL OZ) BUTTERMILK

1 Preheat the oven to 190°C/375°F/gas mark 5 and lightly oil a baking sheet.

2 Sift the flours, salt, bicarbonate of soda, and cream of tartar into a large bowl. Rub in the butter until the mixture resembles bread crumbs. Stir in the sugar and make a well in the centre. Mix in enough of the buttermilk to make a soft dough. Do not overwork the dough – it will become heavy if you do.

3 Shape the dough into a round and place it on the baking sheet. Using the handle of a wooden spoon dipped in flour, make a deep cross in the dough (*see* page 165).

4 Dust the dough lightly with wholemeal flour and bake it for 30–35 minutes, until it has risen and the base sounds hollow when tapped with your fingertips. Cool it on a wire rack.

note

If you cannot find buttermilk in the shops, make a close equivalent at home. Mix 1 tbsp lemon juice (or cider vinegar) to 225ml (8fl oz) skimmed milk. Stir and let it stand for about 5 minutes, then use.

BAKING: 35–40 minutes   **MAKES:** 1 loaf

red pepper and chilli polenta bread

THIS SPICY AND LIGHT IMPROMPTU BREAD IS GREAT TO SERVE WITH SOUP. IT'S COLOURFUL, AS WELL, AND YOU CAN ADAPT THE RECIPE TO INCLUDE OTHER INGREDIENTS – MORE CHILLI IF YOU ARE INCLINED TOWARDS HEAT, SOME CHEESE, WHATEVER YOU FANCY. THE BUTTERMILK OR YOGURT GIVES THE BREAD A LIGHT TEXTURE.

1 Preheat the oven to 190°C/ 375°F/gas mark 5. Butter a 25 x 16cm (10 x 6¼in) baking tin.

2 Mix the semolina or polenta, flour, and bicarbonate of soda in a large bowl, seasoning well with salt and pepper. Make a well in the centre.

3 Thoroughly mix the remaining ingredients in a jug.

4 Pour the wet ingredients onto the dry ones and stir lightly to combine them. Do not overstir, because this will cause the bread to be tough.

5 Pour the mixture into the tin and bake for 35–40 minutes, until the bread is firm and golden. Cool it a little on a wire rack, cut it into squares, and serve warm.

280G (10OZ) FINE SEMOLINA OR POLENTA

85G (3OZ) PLAIN FLOUR

2 TSP BICARBONATE OF SODA

SEA SALT AND FRESHLY GROUND BLACK PEPPER

1 LARGE EGG

150ML (5FL OZ) MILK

425ML (15FL OZ) BUTTERMILK OR
    NATURAL YOGURT

2 LARGE RED CHILLIES, DESEEDED AND
    FINELY CHOPPED

1 RED PEPPER, DESEEDED AND FINELY CHOPPED

pies, tarts, and leftovers

THE ITALIANS LOVE BREAD AND SEE IT AS A PRECIOUS FOOD. CONSEQUENTLY, THEY TRY NOT TO WASTE ANY AND ITALIAN COOKING IS FULL OF FRUGAL RECIPES AND WAYS OF USING UP WHAT IS LEFT OVER. MY GRANDMOTHER, WHO HAD SUCH AN INFLUENCE ON MY COOKING, USED TO SAY THAT IF I WAS CAREFUL, "ONE DAY YOU'LL BE ABLE TO AFFORD A FERRARI." WELL, I HAVEN'T YET BEEN ABLE TO TREAT MYSELF TO SUCH AN EXPENSIVE CAR, BUT I AM DEFINITELY CAREFUL — WITH MY INGREDIENTS AND WITH MY TIME.

I OFTEN MAKE TWICE AS MUCH DOUGH AS I NEED; I WILL USE HALF TO MAKE MY BREAD, BUT THE OTHER HALF I USE TO MAKE THE CASING FOR A PIE, INSTEAD OF USING PASTRY. THIS IS A VERY ITALIAN THING TO DO AND IT'S USEFUL FOR PICNICS BECAUSE BREAD DOUGH BAKES TO A MORE SOLID CRUST THAN PASTRY, SO THE PIE IS MORE LIKELY TO REACH ITS DESTINATION IN ONE PIECE. THE TEXTURE IS INTERESTING, TOO, REMAINING CRISPER THAN MANY PASTRIES DO. THE IDEA WORKS BEST WITH AN EGG-ENRICHED DOUGH, SUCH AS THE PITTA ON PAGE 47.

I ALSO USE UP LEFTOVERS. YOU CAN MAKE A QUICK SNACK LUNCH OR A CASUAL STARTER FROM A COUPLE OF SLICES OF *BRUSCHETTA* WITH A TOPPING; YOU CAN MAKE *CROSTINI* TO SERVE WITH SOUPS; YOU CAN PUT BITS OF DAY-OLD BREAD IN SOUPS OR SALADS; AND YOU CAN EVEN USE LEFTOVER OR SLIGHTLY STALE BREAD IN PUDDINGS.

THE MOST USEFUL ROLE OF LEFTOVER BREAD, HOWEVER, IS AS BREAD CRUMBS. THEY CAN BE FRESH OR DRIED (PUT THE BREAD IN THE OVEN ON A LOW HEAT UNTIL IT IS CRISP, THEN CRUSH IT); THE FRESH CAN BE FROZEN AND THE DRIED CAN BE STORED IN AN AIRTIGHT CONTAINER. THERE ARE NO BREAD CRUMB RECIPES HERE — I DON'T THINK YOU NEED ANY! — BUT I USE FRESH BREAD CRUMBS TO BULK OUT MEAT FOR MEATBALLS; TO COAT CUTLETS, FISH, OR VEGETABLES BEFORE FRYING, GRILLING, OR BAKING THEM; OR AS A TOPPING. I SOMETIMES MIX CHOPPED FRESH HERBS WITH BREAD CRUMBS (THIS TASTES WONDERFUL SPRINKLED ON TOP OF A FISH PIE BEFORE IT IS BAKED), AND FRESHLY GRATED PARMESAN WITH BREAD CRUMBS MAKES A FANTASTIC COATING FOR FRESH TUNA OR A TOPPING FOR GRATINS.

olive and anchovy savoury pie

THIS PIE IS FROM PUGLIA IN ITALY, WHERE THE FLAVOURS OF OLIVES AND ANCHOVIES DOMINATE THE CUISINE.
IT IS EATEN DURING LENT AND THE FILLINGS CAN VARY: I LOVE ASPARAGUS, BASIL, AND PARMESAN.

1 To make the dough, mix the flour and salt in a large bowl. Make a well in the centre and add half the oil. Dissolve the yeast in a little of the water and add it to the well. Mix with a wooden spoon, adding the remaining water bit by bit until a soft dough is formed.

2 Knead the dough on a lightly floured surface for 5 minutes. Divide it into 5 equal portions, cover with a damp tea towel, and leave to rise for 45 minutes.

3 Oil a 20cm (8in) springform cake tin. Roll the first piece of dough into a 20cm (8in) circle. Transfer it to the tin to cover the base.

4 Mix the anchovies, olives, and parsley well. Spread the base of the dough with a quarter of this mixture and drizzle the surface

with oil. Roll the second piece of dough into a 20cm (8in) circle and arrange it in the tin on top of the filling. Spread a third of the remaining anchovy mixture over it. Continue like this, rolling three more 20cm (8in) dough circles, until all the ingredients have been used, ending with a top layer of dough.

5 Brush the top with oil and pierce it with a fork in a few places, then cover and leave to prove for 20 minutes.

6 Preheat the oven to 200°C/ 400°F/gas mark 6.

7 Bake for 40 minutes. Remove from the oven and allow to cool on a wire rack. Cut it into tiny wedges (it is very rich and filling) and serve hot or cold.

DOUGH

300G (10½OZ) STRONG WHITE FLOUR

1 TSP FINE SEA SALT

2 TBSP OLIVE OIL

10G (¼OZ) FRESH YEAST, CRUMBLED

100ML (3½FL OZ) WATER AT BODY TEMPERATURE

FILLING

26 SALTED ANCHOVIES, RINSED AND DICED

200G (7OZ) OLIVES (ANY TYPE), STONED

A HANDFUL OF FRESH FLAT-LEAF PARSLEY LEAVES, FINELY CHOPPED

3 TBSP OLIVE OIL

cheese, egg, and pepper pie

THIS IS A YEASTED BREAD PIE FROM CALABRIA IN SOUTHERN ITALY. MY VERSION OF IT IS FILLED WITH CHEESE AND PEPPERS, BUT HAM AND BACON ARE OTHER POPULAR FILLINGS. I'VE SUGGESTED CACIOCAVALLO CHEESE, BUT IF YOU CANNOT BUY IT, YOU COULD USE PROVOLONE OR EXTRA RICOTTA INSTEAD.

DOUGH

300G (10½OZ) STRONG WHITE FLOUR

FINE SEA SALT AND FRESHLY GROUND
    BLACK PEPPER

15G (½OZ) FRESH YEAST, CRUMBLED

6 TBSP WATER AT BODY TEMPERATURE

2 LARGE EGGS

20G (¾OZ) UNSALTED BUTTER

1 TBSP OLIVE OIL

FILLING

2 RED PEPPERS

115G (4OZ) CACIOCAVALLO CHEESE

2 LARGE EGGS, HARD-BOILED AND SHELLED

200G (7OZ) RICOTTA CHEESE

1 Preheat the oven to 200°C/ 400°F/gas mark 6.

2 Sift half the flour and a pinch of salt into a bowl, and make a well in the centre. Cream the fresh yeast with 4 tbsp of the water, then add it to the well in the flour with the remaining water. Mix well to form a smooth dough. Shape it into a ball, cover with a damp tea towel, and leave to rise in a warm place for 1 hour.

3 Meanwhile, for the filling, put the peppers on a baking sheet and roast for 20 minutes, until they are deflated and slightly charred, turning them as they cook. Leave them to cool, then skin them and roughly chop the flesh. Slice the caciocavallo cheese and hard-boiled eggs.

4 When the dough has risen, beat the eggs and melt the butter. Sift the remaining flour onto a work surface and work it into the risen dough with the eggs, butter, and oil. Knead until it is smooth: about 10 minutes.

5 On a lightly floured surface, roll out two thirds of the dough to fit a 23cm (9in) cake tin, letting the dough come up the sides. Arrange the cheese and egg slices, sprinkled with salt and pepper, the ricotta, and the peppers, in the tin.

6 Roll out the remaining dough to a circle to make a lid and arrange it over the filling. Fold the edges inward, pressing them together to seal them. Cover the pie and leave it to prove in a warm place for 30 minutes.

7 Brush the top with extra olive oil. Bake for 30 minutes, until the pie is golden. Serve warm.

RISING: 1 hour   **PROVING:** 30 minutes   **BAKING:** 30–35 minutes   **DRIED YEAST:** 2 tsp   **MAKES:** 1 pie (to serve 6)

savoury spinach pie

THIS PIE IS USUALLY EATEN ON MAY DAY IN ITALY BECAUSE THE SPINACH REPRESENTS ALL THE FRESH GREENERY
THAT IS AROUND AT THAT TIME OF YEAR. IT COULD ALSO HAVE OTHER SOFT-LEAVED GREENS IN IT, SUCH AS HERBS.
IT IS A GOOD PIE TO TAKE ON A PICNIC.

1 Put the spinach in a large pot, cover, and cook in its own water over a medium heat for 5 minutes or until it has wilted. Drain, cool, and form it into 4 balls, squeezing each ball until it is dry. Chop the spinach balls and set them aside.

2 Heat the butter in a frying pan over a low heat. Add the pancetta, garlic, and spring onions and sauté for 8 minutes, stirring constantly. Add the spinach and cook for 5 minutes, stirring all the ingredients until they are well blended. Season and set aside.

3 Butter and flour a 20cm (8in) springform cake tin and place it on a baking sheet. Divide the dough into two portions, one slightly larger than the other. Put the larger portion on a floured surface and roll it into a 25cm (10in) circle that is 3mm (⅛in) thick. Place the circle into the springform tin, patting the dough up and against the sides.

4 Top with the spinach mixture, smoothing the surface with a spatula. Beat the eggs with the cheese and pour over the spinach.

5 Roll out the remaining portion of dough into a 20cm (8in) circle that is 3mm (⅛in) thick. Cover the filling with this small circle, pressing the edges of the dough to seal them shut. Pierce the top with a fork in three or four places. Cover the pie and leave it to prove in a warm place for 30 minutes.

6 Preheat the oven to 180°C/ 350°F/gas mark 4.

7 Bake the pie for 30–35 minutes or until the surface of the dough is golden brown. Cool it slightly, then remove from the pan. Cut into wedges and garnish with cherry-tomato halves.

1 RECIPE PITTA DOUGH, RISEN (*SEE* PAGE 47)

6 CHERRY TOMATOES ON THE VINE, HALVED

FILLING

1.5KG (3LB 5OZ) FRESH SPINACH, TOUGH STALKS REMOVED, WASHED, AND LEFT WET

55G (2OZ) UNSALTED BUTTER

85G (3OZ) PANCETTA, FINELY CHOPPED

1 GARLIC CLOVE, PEELED AND FINELY CHOPPED

6 SPRING ONIONS, FINELY CHOPPED

SEA SALT AND FRESHLY GROUND BLACK PEPPER

2 LARGE EGGS

150G (5½OZ) PARMESAN, FRESHLY GRATED

chard and ricotta tart

THIS TASTY TART IS A LIGURIAN SPECIALITY EATEN AT EASTER. IT USED TO BE MADE WITH MORE THAN 30 LAYERS OF PASTRY, TO CELEBRATE THE YEARS OF CHRIST'S LIFE, BUT MY VERSION IS SOMEWHAT LIGHTER. THE CASING IS NOT A BREAD DOUGH, BUT IT IS OILY DOUGH, WHICH MAKES FOR AN INTERESTINGLY CRISP TEXTURE.

1 Heap the flour on a work surface and make a well in the centre. Add the oil, salt, and most of the water and stir with a fork, incorporating a little flour each time and adding water to create a smooth, elastic dough. Some flour may remain. Divide the dough into 10 balls, each the size of an egg. Cover with a damp tea towel and set aside to rest for 20 minutes.

2 Blanch the chard in boiling salted water for 3–4 minutes, until it wilts. Cool it to room temperature, squeeze dry, and chop finely.

3 Heat 1 tbsp of oil in a frying pan over a medium heat and sauté the onion for 3–4 minutes, until it is translucent. Strain the mushrooms, chop, and add them and the chard to the onion. Sauté for 7 minutes, stirring constantly. Remove from the heat and set aside.

4 Put the ricotta, milk, bread, and a pinch of salt in a bowl, and mix.

5 Preheat the oven to 180°C/ 350°F/gas mark 4. Butter and flour a 25cm (10in) springform cake tin.

6 Put the dough on a floured work surface and roll each ball into a 25cm (10in) circle. Place one on the bottom of the pan and brush with some of the remaining oil. Layer with four more circles, brushing each with oil.

7 Spread the fifth layer with the chard mixture. Cover with the sixth layer of dough and spread this with the ricotta mixture. Make six egg-sized depressions in the ricotta and break an egg into each. Sprinkle the Parmesan over them.

8 Layer the remaining dough in the pan, brushing each circle with oil. Pierce the top once or twice with a fork and brush with oil.

9 Bake for 1 hour or until golden brown. Serve in wedges either cold or at room temperature.

DOUGH

300G (10½OZ) ITALIAN "00" PLAIN FLOUR

4 TBSP OLIVE OIL

2 TSP FINE SEA SALT

2–3 TBSP WATER

FILLING

1.5KG (3LB 5OZ) SWISS CHARD, STEMMED

4 TBSP OLIVE OIL

1 SMALL ONION, PEELED AND DICED

75G (2¾OZ) DRIED PORCINI, SOAKED IN WATER FOR 20 MINUTES

500G (18OZ) FRESH RICOTTA CHEESE

200ML (7FL OZ) FULL-FAT MILK

2 SLICES COUNTRY BREAD, CRUSTS REMOVED

SEA SALT AND FRESHLY GROUND BLACK PEPPER

6 LARGE EGGS

125G (4½OZ) PARMESAN, FRESHLY GRATED

country-style cheese and ham pie

THIS CLASSIC PIE HAILS FROM ONE OF MY FAVOURITE REGIONS OF ITALY, PUGLIA, AND THE RECIPE COMES DIRECTLY FROM MY FRIENDS IN LECCE. IT'S A CLASSIC EXAMPLE OF THE REGION'S LOVE OF THIS COMBINATION OF INGREDIENTS.

DOUGH

1 RECIPE PITTA DOUGH (*SEE* PAGE 47, BUT
   SEE ALSO STEP 1 ON THIS PAGE), RISEN

A HANDFUL OF FRESH FLAT-LEAF PARSLEY
   LEAVES, CHOPPED

2 TSP COARSELY GROUND BLACK PEPPER

FILLING

1–2 TBSP OLIVE OIL

200G (7OZ) PARMA HAM, CUT INTO
   1CM (½IN) CUBES

225G (8OZ) BUFFALO MOZZARELLA,
   CUT INTO 1CM (½IN) CUBES

225G (8OZ) RICOTTA CHEESE

200G (7OZ) CACIOCAVALLO, YOUNG PECORINO,
   OR PROVOLONE CHEESE

2 LARGE EGGS, LIGHTLY BEATEN

SEA SALT AND FRESHLY GROUND BLACK PEPPER

1 When making the dough as on page 47, beat in the herbs and pepper at the same time as the eggs and melted butter.

2 To make the filling, heat the oil in a frying pan and sauté the ham for 4 minutes. Put it into a bowl to cool. Add the three cheeses, eggs, and some salt and pepper, and mix until well blended. Set aside.

3 Flour a 25cm (10in) springform cake tin. Divide the dough into two portions, one being three quarters of the dough. Put the large portion on a floured surface and roll it into a 30cm (12in) circle that is 1cm (½in) thick. Place it into the tin, patting the dough up and against the sides. Place the filling on top of the dough. Roll out the remaining dough into a 25cm (10in) square with a thickness of 1cm (½in). Cut it

into 2.5cm- (1in-) wide strips and arrange them as a latticework on top of the filling. Cover the pie and leave it to prove in a warm place for 30 minutes.

4 Preheat the oven to 190°C/ 375°F/gas mark 5.

5 Bake the pie for 45 minutes or until the pastry is golden brown. Remove from the oven, cut into wedges, and serve hot or cold.

bruschetta

BRUSCHETTE ARE SLICES OF RUSTIC BREAD, BAKED UNTIL THEY ARE CRISP AND SLIGHTLY CHARRED, AND THEN RUBBED WITH GARLIC AND DRIZZLED WITH OLIVE OIL. THEY ARE A PARTICULAR TREAT IF YOU ARE IN ITALY IN NOVEMBER, WHEN THEY ARE MADE WITH THE NEWLY PRESSED OIL. USUALLY SERVED AS AN APPETIZER, *BRUSCHETTE* ARE ALSO VERY GOOD WITH FISH SOUPS AND PAN-FRIED CHICKEN LIVERS. THEY CAN BE TOPPED, AS WELL — SEE THE NEXT TWO RECIPES.

6 LARGE SLICES OPEN-TEXTURED ITALIAN BREAD, ABOUT 1.5CM (⅝IN) THICK
2 GARLIC CLOVES, PEELED AND HALVED
ABOUT 6 TBSP EXTRA VIRGIN OLIVE OIL
SEA SALT AND FRESHLY GROUND BLACK PEPPER

1 Preheat the grill or a griddle pan and preheat the oven to 220°C/425°F/gas mark 7.

2 Score the bread slices lightly with the point of a small knife in a criss-cross fashion, then grill or griddle them to toast them on both sides.

3 While the bread is still hot, rub one toasted surface of each slice all over with the cut garlic cloves. Put the toast slices on a baking sheet and bake them in the oven for 2 minutes to crisp them through.

4 Drizzle about 1 tbsp of extra virgin olive oil over each slice. Sprinkle generously with pepper and a little salt, then serve.

variation

Crostini are much smaller and more elegant, rather like the French *croûtes.* In a *trattoria,* for instance, I would be offered a *bruschetta;* in a *ristorante,* a *crostino. Crostini* are usually grilled like *bruschette,* but they can be baked in the oven until they are crisp. They are good with salads, soups, as canapés, and for dipping.

caramelized fennel, onion, and olive bruschetta

FENNEL IS NATIVE TO ITALY, WHERE IT IS EATEN RAW TO AID DIGESTION. IF ANYONE REMAINS UNCONVINCED BY FENNEL'S CHARMS, THIS IS THE RECIPE TO CONVERT THEM, BECAUSE THE FLAVOUR OF THE FENNEL IS MUTED AND SWEETENED BY THE COOKING. THIS VERSION GIVES ONLY ONE EXAMPLE OF A POSSIBLE *BRUSCHETTA* TOPPING, AND THERE'S ANOTHER ON PAGE 180, BUT YOU CAN LET YOUR IMAGINATION RUN WILD AND CREATE MANY TOPPINGS OF YOUR OWN.

1 Melt the butter and olive oil in a non-stick, heavy-bottomed pan. Stir in the sliced onion and fennel and stew slowly for about 45 minutes, stirring from time to time, until the vegetables are golden brown and tender.

2 Add the wine and olives and continue cooking until the wine has bubbled away completely. Adjust the seasoning and keep the mixture warm.

3 Grill the bread until it is golden brown. Spoon the warm fennel mixture over it and serve at once.

variation

Any topping could be used for a *bruschetta:* walnut or rocket pesto, an olive tapenade, taramasalata or hummus, *peperonata* (roasted peppers), *caponata* (see page 88), chicken liver pâté, sliced tomatoes…

15G (½OZ) UNSALTED BUTTER

1 TBSP OLIVE OIL

2 ONIONS, PEELED AND FINELY SLICED

2 FENNEL BULBS, TRIMMED, QUARTERED, AND FINELY SLICED

50ML (2FL OZ) WHITE WINE

8 BLACK OLIVES, STONED AND SLICED

SEA SALT AND FRESHLY GROUND BLACK PEPPER

4 LARGE SLICES OPEN-TEXTURED BREAD, CUT 1CM (½IN) THICK

cavolo nero and bean bruschetta

BEANS AND *CAVOLO NERO* (BLACK CABBAGE) GO WELL TOGETHER — WHICH MAY SURPRISE YOU — BUT IT IS THE QUALITY OF THE OIL THAT BRINGS THIS DISH TOGETHER AND CREATES THE SIMPLEST POSSIBLE TOPPING FOR *BRUSCHETTA*. DO TRY TO COOK YOUR OWN BEANS, BECAUSE THEY WILL TASTE SO MUCH BETTER.

6 SLICES *BRUSCHETTA* (*SEE* PAGE 178)

450G (1LB) *CAVOLO NERO*

SEA SALT AND FRESHLY GROUND BLACK PEPPER

200G (7OZ) COOKED CANNELLINI BEANS

THE BEST POSSIBLE EXTRA VIRGIN OLIVE OIL

1 Cut the *cavolo nero* into 5cm (2in) pieces, and cook in a saucepan of boiling salted water for about 10–15 minutes, until tender. Drain well.

2 Meanwhile, heat up the beans in a small saucepan.

3 When the *bruschetta* slices are ready, put them on plates, garlic-side up, and top first with the *cavolo nero,* then with the beans. The finishing touch is the glorious oil, along with a sprinkling of salt and pepper. Eat immediately.

reboiled soup

TUSCANS COOK *LA RIBOLLITA* WITH *CAVOLO NERO,* A BLACK CABBAGE THAT COMES INTO SEASON JUST AS THE NEW OLIVE OIL IS PRESSED IN NOVEMBER. THE OIL IS AN IMPORTANT ELEMENT AND SHOULD NOT BE OVERLOOKED. MAKE AS MUCH OF THIS SOUP AS FITS COMFORTABLY IN YOUR LARGEST CASSEROLE — THE QUANTITIES BELOW ARE SIMPLY A BASIC GUIDE. LIKE MANY OTHER SOUPS, IT IMPROVES IF IT IS LEFT FOR A DAY — THUS THE NAME.

1 Soak the cannellini beans overnight in cold water. Drain and rinse them.

2 Sweat the onion in a large flameproof casserole in half of the oil. Add the carrot, celery, leek, *cavolo nero,* and tomatoes and mix so they are liberally covered in oil. Add half the garlic and all the chilli and cook for 10 minutes.

3 Add the soaked beans and stir. Cover with water and then simmer slowly, covered, for 1½-2 hours or until the beans are soft.

4 Remove a third of the soup mixture and mash or liquidize it to a purée. Return it to the casserole.

5 In a separate pan, warm the remaining oil and sauté the remaining minced garlic with the herbs until it is lightly brown. Add to the casserole and leave for 24 hours.

6 The next day, warm the mixture through, uncovered. It should be wet but not sloppy. Season to taste. Lay a slice of bread on the bottom of a soup bowl, ladle the soup over it, and then pour over a generous amount — don't stint — of extra virgin olive oil, with a sprinkling of salt and parsley.

175G (6OZ) DRIED CANNELLINI BEANS

1 LARGE ONION, PEELED AND SLICED

4 TBSP OLIVE OIL

4 CARROTS, PEELED AND CHOPPED

4 CELERY STALKS, TRIMMED AND CHOPPED

4 LEEKS, WASHED, TRIMMED AND CHOPPED

250G (9OZ) *CAVOLO NERO,* TRIMMED AND WASHED

8 TOMATOES, SKINNED, QUARTERED, AND SEEDED

2 GARLIC CLOVES, PEELED AND MINCED

1 DRIED CHILLI (*PEPERONCINO*), CRUMBLED, SEEDS AND ALL

A HANDFUL OF FRESH HERBS (PARSLEY, BAY, AND ROSEMARY), CHOPPED

SEA SALT AND FRESHLY GROUND BLACK PEPPER

8 SLICES COUNTRY-STYLE BREAD

NEW-SEASON EXTRA VIRGIN OLIVE OIL

3 TBSP CHOPPED FRESH FLAT-LEAF PARSLEY

SERVES: 6

tuscan tomato soup

THIS IS A CLASSIC SOUP FROM THE MAREMMA REGION OF SOUTHERN TUSCANY. IT IS USUALLY MADE WITH ONIONS, CELERY, GARLIC, TOMATOES, BREAD, AND BOILING WATER – IT IS CALLED *ACQUACOTTA,* OR "COOKED WATER", IN ITALIAN – BUT THERE ARE MANY VARIATIONS. MOST OF THESE INVOLVE EGG: YOU CAN POACH THE EGGS IN THE TOMATO BASE BEFORE ADDING THE BOILING WATER, OR YOU CAN BEAT EGGS WITH GRATED PARMESAN AND STIR THEM IN, RATHER LIKE A *STRACCIATELLA.* I HAVE OMITTED EGGS FROM THIS VERSION, BUT YOU CAN ADD THEM IF YOU WANT TO. THE OIL USED AT THE END SHOULD BE THE BEST YOU CAN OBTAIN.

2 TBSP GOOD OLIVE OIL

250G (9OZ) WHITE ONIONS, PEELED AND SLICED

2 CELERY STALKS, FINELY CHOPPED

2 CARROTS, SCRUBBED AND FINELY CHOPPED

2 GARLIC CLOVES, PEELED AND CRUSHED

500G (18OZ) FRESH PLUM TOMATOES

6 MEDIUM SLICES FIRM, COARSE-TEXTURED BREAD

1.5 LITRES (2¼ PINTS) BOILING WATER

SEA SALT AND FRESHLY GROUND BLACK PEPPER

3 TBSP CHOPPED FRESH FLAT-LEAF PARSLEY

6 TBSP FRUITY EXTRA VIRGIN OLIVE OIL

1 Heat the olive oil in a large saucepan and cook the onions over a moderate heat until they are translucent. Add the celery, carrot, and garlic and cook for a few minutes more.

2 Put the tomatoes through a mouli or sieve or grate them directly into the saucepan, stir, and simmer over a low heat for 20–30 minutes to thicken the tomatoes.

3 Meanwhile, toast the slices of bread and put each in the bottom of a serving bowl.

4 Add the boiling water to the tomato mixture, season with salt and pepper, and simmer for 6–10 minutes more.

5 Pour the soup over the bread in bowls and stand for about 5 minutes to allow the bread to absorb the flavours. Serve hot, sprinkled with parsley and with a drizzle of that glorious olive oil.

bread and mozzarella salad

A BREAD SALAD MAY APPEAR SIMPLE BUT IT'S DELICIOUS. HOWEVER, IT IS VITAL THAT YOU USE THE BEST POSSIBLE BASIC INGREDIENTS – BREAD, TOMATOES, MOZZARELLA, AND BASIL. THEN YOU CAN ADD EXTRAS TO YOUR HEART'S CONTENT – SOME MORE GARLIC AND OLIVES, FOR INSTANCE, OR SOME GOOD CAPERS.

1 Tear the bread into small chunks. Combine them with the tomatoes, mozzarella, basil, oregano, garlic, olives, and salt and pepper to taste.

2 Drizzle generously with olive oil. Mix well and serve.

450G (1LB) SLIGHTLY DRY, FIRM-TEXTURED, COUNTRY BREAD

2 RIPE TOMATOES, DESEEDED AND DICED

450G (1LB) BUFFALO MOZZARELLA CHEESE, TORN INTO 1CM (½IN) PIECES

A HANDFUL OF FRESH BASIL LEAVES, TORN

1 TSP DRIED OREGANO

1 GARLIC CLOVE, PEELED AND CRUSHED

A HANDFUL OF BLACK OLIVES, STONED

SEA SALT AND FRESHLY GROUND BLACK PEPPER

125ML (4FL OZ) BOLD, FRUITY EXTRA VIRGIN OLIVE OIL

fruit bread-and-butter pudding

BREAD-AND-BUTTER PUDDING IS A BRITISH CLASSIC, BUT USING A GERMAN OR AUSTRIAN FRUIT LOAF INSTEAD OF *BRIOCHE* (FRENCH) OR *PANETTONE* (ITALIAN) GIVES IT A NEW SLANT. THIS PUDDING RECIPE DOESN'T CONTAIN ANY SUGAR BECAUSE THE BREAD IS SWEET ENOUGH ALREADY.

1–2 SMALL ALPINE FRUIT BREADS (*SEE* PAGE 136)

ABOUT 55G (2OZ) UNSALTED BUTTER, MELTED

2 LARGE EGGS

150ML (5FL OZ) FULL-FAT MILK

3 TBSP DOUBLE CREAM

1 TSP VANILLA EXTRACT

1 Cut the bread into 1cm (½in) thick slices and butter generously.

2 Grease a shallow baking dish of about 30 x 20cm (12 x 8in) with some extra butter and arrange the slices of bread in it, overlapping them like fish scales.

3 Whisk the remaining ingredients together well, then pour this custard over the bread. Leave it to soak for half an hour.

4 Preheat the oven to 180°C/ 350°F/gas mark 4.

5 Bake the pudding for 15–20 minutes. Serve it warm with extra cream if needed.

variation

For added sweetness – if you want or need any – you could spread the buttered slices of bread with some marmalade.

brown-bread ice cream

THE BREAD NEEDN'T NECESSARILY BE BROWN, BECAUSE TOASTING THE CRUMBS OF ANY BREAD BROWNS AND FLAVOURS THEM. THE BREADS YOU COULD USE FROM THIS BOOK INCLUDE THE *PAIN DE CAMPAGNE* (*SEE* PAGE 30), THE GRANARY (*SEE* PAGE 33), AND EVEN THE WALNUT BREAD (*SEE* PAGE 46).

1 Preheat the oven to 200°C/400°F/gas mark 6. Spread the bread crumbs over a baking sheet and put it into the oven for about 5 minutes, stirring the crumbs around occasionally. Watch carefully, because they can quickly catch and burn. Remove from the oven and keep them handy.

2 Meanwhile, heat the sugar and water together to melt the sugar, then simmer to form a syrup, until it begins to brown around the edges. Take the syrup off the heat and stir it into the toasted bread crumbs to coat them well. Put the caramel-coated crumbs on a piece of greaseproof paper on a baking tray and leave to set. Then crumble into smaller pieces in your hands.

3 Whip the cream to soft peaks, then fold in the icing sugar, vanilla, and spirit of choice, followed by the breadcrumbs.

4 Pour into a 900ml (1½pint) freezerproof container and freeze overnight. Rest for half an hour or so in the fridge before serving.

115G (4OZ) FRESH BREAD CRUMBS

115G (4OZ) GOLDEN GRANULATED SUGAR

90ML (3FL OZ) WATER

500ML (18FL OZ) WHIPPING CREAM

70G (2½OZ) ICING SUGAR

1 TSP VANILLA EXTRACT

2 TBSP BRANDY, RUM, OR WHISKY

index

acknowledgments

To Bridget Colvin, my great friend, who has contributed recipe-wise and cerebrally throughout the development of this book: Thank you also for the use of your house for the photoshoot. You are an amazing cook and recipe developer, and your knowledge and dedication are extraordinary. Thank you. Thank you!

To Susan Fleming, who edited the book: You are always such fun to work with and your outstanding drive and passion to get it right thrill me.

To Simon Wheeler, photographer: You have been the best thing to happen to me over this past year. I'm a huge fan of your work and this book is a shining example. I am very happy. Thank you.

To Jonathan Brunton, photography assistant: A great talent and someone to look out for.

To Geoff Borin, designer: I'm thrilled that you worked on my book – you've done a beautiful job.

To Rebecca Spry, commissioning editor: Clever, hardworking, delightful, and determined.

To Suzanne Arnold, senior editor: Thank you for shaping everything up and for your fine eye, determining the best.

To Richard Moore, my husband and chief taster.

To Rosie Kindersley and Eric Treuille: I love working with Books for Cooks. You are a great source of inspiration, always.

Thank you all.

Ursula

The publishers would like to thank Dany Mitzman for her assistance.